Hope Bourne's
EXMOOR
Eloquence In Art
By John Burgess with Caroline Tonson-Rye

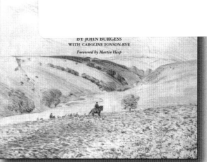

**£24.99, ISBN 978 0 85704 218 7,
hardback, 214x230mm, 144 pages**

HOPE BOURNE has been described as one of the finest writers about the British countryside in the twentieth century. In beautifully measured terms, she described the daily round of a life lived close to nature and to the land. Her work published in her lifetime invariably included some supporting line drawings – sharply memorable vignettes – and full-colour works for the covers of her books, for she was an extremely skilled artist. Yet although she left over 2000 artworks at her death, and many others in private hands, there has hitherto not been a volume that focuses on her painting and drawing.

Now for the first time, the publication of a collection of her works of art gives the opportunity to remedy this omission and to view Hope Bourne and her achievements through the media of her paint-box and her pencil.

With a carefully selected text, some of it drawn from her unpublished writing, and an expert commentary from John Burgess, with Caroline Tonson-Rye, *Hope Bourne's Exmoor* redresses the balance in our appreciation of this remarkable figure. It allows us to savour just how eloquent Hope Bourne could be in her visual record as well as in her prose. Her sketches, with pencilled comments, show her acute observation of colour and light through the seasons. As the remarkable pictures in this book show, she understood Exmoor in all its moods and her work is imbued utterly with the spirit of the place.

ALSO AVAILABLE BY HOPE BOURNE:

Jael
Legendary country writer
Hope Bourne's only novel.
£12.99, 978 0 85704 089 3,
hardback, 160 pages

A Moorland Year
£12.95, 978 0 86183 253 8, hardback, 192 pages

Wild Harvest
£12.95, 978 0 86183 431 0, hardback, 136 pages

Available from local stockists throughout the area or, in case of difficulty, from
**Halsgrove Publishing, Halsgrove House, Ryelands Business Park, Bagley Road,
Wellington, Somerset TA21 9PZ.**
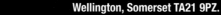
Tel: 01823 653777, e-mail: sales@halsgrove.com, www.halsgrove.com

2

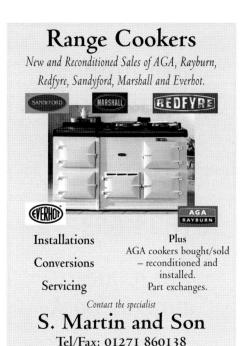

A SMALL SELECTION OF HALSGROVE'S SUPERB BOOKS* COVERING EXMOOR AND WEST SOMERSET

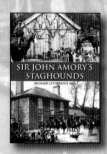

**A Singular Exmoor Man –
Hector Heywood**
£19.99, hardback, 160 pages

Sir John Amory's Staghounds
£24.99, hardback, 160 pages

**Peter Heard's Paintings of a
West Country Life**
£14.99, hardback, 144 pages

Donald Ayres' Exmoor Revisited
£24.99, hardback, 144 pages

**REPRINTED AND UPDATED
Exmoor Rangers'
Favourite Walks**
£6.99, paperback, 112 pages

Exmoor Address Book
£12.99, Peter Hendrie,
hardback, 112 pages

West Somerset in the News
£19.99, Jeff Cox,
hardback, 160 pages

The Overland Launch
£9.99, C. Walter Hodges,
hardback, 112 pages

Exmoor – A Winter's Tale
£14.99, Neville Stanikk,
hardback, 144 pages

The West Somerset Railway
£12.99, Don Bishop,
hardback, 144 pages

**The West Somerset
Railway Revisited**
£16.99, Don Bishop,
hardback, 144 pages

**Spirit of the West
Somerset Railway**
£4.99, Don Bishop,
hardback, 64 pages

An Exmoor Panorama
£24.99, Peter Hendrie,
hardback, 144 pages

Spirit of Exmoor
£4.99, Peter Hendrie,
hardback, 64 pages

**Somerset Cricket –
The Glory Years, 1973-1987**
£19.99, Alain Lockyer and Richard
Walsh, hardback, 144 pages

Perfect Exmoor
£14.99, Neville Stanikk,
hardback, 144 pages

**NEW
Another Somerset Century**
£12.99, Charles Wood,
hardback, 168 pages

Exmoor Amour
12.99, Charles Wood,
hardback, 168 pages

**Charles Wood's Somerset
Quiz Book**
£8.99, paperback, 96 pages

**Surviving Another
Somerset Year**
£12.99, Charles Wood,
hardback, 160 pages

Bats, Pads and Cider
£12.99, Charles Wood,
hardback, 160 pages

**Village Schooling in Somerset –
Learn 'em Hard**
£24.99, Sarah Villiers,
hardback, 224 pages

The Last Word on Exmoor
£12.99, Norma Huxtable,
hardback, 144 pages

PHOTO E. ASKEW

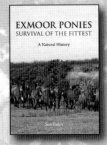
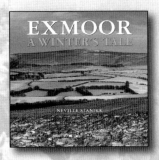
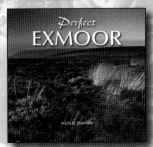

Guardians of the Breed

A registered Charity, the Exmoor Pony Society was set up in 1921 for the registration of pure-bred Exmoor ponies, the conservation of the breed and the preservation of the breed standard as well as promoting the ponies to the general public. The Society holds the official stud book and, in accordance, with DEFRA legislation acts as a Passport Issuing Organisation. The Society has worked with the Exmoor National Park Authority and the Rare Breed Survival Trust for many years to ensure that the Exmoor Pony, which remains on the Rare Breed Survival Trust's Watchlist in Category 2, survives both in its natural habitat and away from the moor. More recently the Society has worked with the Exmoor Moorland Landscape Partnership on initiatives such as the Exmoor Pony Festival.

The Society is grateful to all its members, both on and off Exmoor, together with those members of the public who provide information about the ponies on the moor during the year and are concerned for their welfare.

You can help too – JOIN THE SOCIETY – Associate Membership is just £17.00 a year.

For more information call our Freefone number 0845 607 5350 or visit our website www.exmoorponysociety.org.uk.

Famous Beers From Exmoor

Stockleigh Lodge
Country House Bed and Breakfast

A beautiful large country house set in its own wooded grounds, within a short walk of the village of Exford, in the centre of Exmoor National Park. With 9 ensuite rooms, with views over the garden it is ideal for small groups for walking, riding or exploring the Park by car. Stabling available for bringing your own horse on holiday. Ample parking. Contact Mike or Myra Ellicott

Prices: per person per night: £35 - £40 Rooms: 9

T: 01643 831500 E: stay@stockleighexford.co.uk
W: www.stockleighexford.co.uk
Exford Exmoor, Somerset TA24 7PZ AA 4 star

Near Brockwell
JENNY GIBSON

EXMOOR

Infinite variety is part of the charm of Exmoor, for the landscape is a mixture of moorlands and vast views, precipitous and spectacular cliffs, deeply incised wooded combes, rolling hills, traditional upland farms and narrow lanes lined with beech hedges connecting picturesque villages, hamlets and farmsteads. A mosaic of habitats supports a great diversity of wildlife, including herds of wild red deer, rich lichen communities, rare fritillary butterflies, and bats. It is an historic landscape that provides a record of how people have lived here since the last ice age. All this is found in a relatively small area of 170,000 acres.

Exmoor's special qualities relate to its distinct landscape, wildlife and cultural heritage. In particular the large areas of open moorland provide a rare sense of remoteness, wildness and tranquillity. It is a farmed landscape with distinctive breeds and a rural community with strong farming traditions. With an exceptional rights of way network and extensive areas of access land it provides superb opportunities for walking, riding and cycling.

A landscape, then, that provides inspiration, livelihoods and prosperity for many but remains fragile and vulnerable to incremental change destroying its unique qualities.

THE EXMOOR SOCIETY

The Exmoor Society was formed in 1958 initially to protest about the proposed afforestation of The Chains and later to save the moorlands from ploughing and fencing. Although successful in these tasks, there are still threats to the moorland today but they are more complex and difficult to solve. There are also new pressures including climate change and its impact on wildlife; increasing recreational demands and development and the loss of rural services and little affordable housing.

We act as an independent champion and watchdog for Exmoor and encourage the understanding of the National Park's special qualities.

We promote responsible enjoyment and access and develop educational and other projects.

We support upland farming and the local economy and community and stimulate public debate on these matters and campaign for sustainable solutions.

We issue free to members a Newsletter in March, an Annual Report in August and the Exmoor Review in October. Our reference library and archives are open to the public.

Join us and help protect Exmoor for all time - *see contact details on next page.*

The Exmoor Society

Registered Charity No 245761

2013 - 2014

President:
Sir Antony Acland KG

Vice Presidents:

Mr Rodney Coyne

Ian Liddell-Grainger, MP

Sir Nicholas Harvey, MP

Baroness Mallalieu, QC

Lord King of Bridgwater, CH PC

Mr Michael Ryle

The Rt. Hon. J.J. Thorpe

Chairman: Mrs Rachel Thomas, CBE DL
Vice-Chairman: Mr Christopher Whinney
Hon. Treasurer: Mrs Karen Trigger, FCA
Hon. Solicitor: Mr Tim Howells, Pardoes
The Society Secretary: Mrs Pat Bawden

Executive Committee:

Mrs Arabella Amory, Tiverton

Mr Christopher Norrish, Clevedon

Mr Chris Binnie, Wootton Courtenay

Miss Jackie Smith, Brompton Regis

Mr John Burgess, Wellington

Mr Mike Taylor, OBE, Alcester, Warwick

Mr Michael Hankin, Minehead

Miss Caroline Tonson-Rye, Dulverton

Dr Duncan Jeffray, Minehead

Mr David Trueman, Barnstaple

Mrs Toni Jones, Dulverton

Dr Richard Westcott, South Molton

Mrs Christina Williams, Molland

Editor of the Exmoor Review: Dr Richard Westcott
Assistant Editor of the Exmoor Review: Mrs Jenny Gibson
Editor of the Spring Newsletter: Mrs Pat Bawden

Chairman, Bristol Group: Mr Christopher Norrish
Acting Chairmen, Barnstaple Group: Mrs Julia Holtom and Mrs Sally Jack
Chairman, Dulverton Group: Mr Peter Donnelly
Chairman, Porlock Group: Dr Duncan Jeffray
Chairman, South Molton Group: Mr George Jones

Office:
Parish Rooms, Dulverton, Somerset TA22 9DP   Tel: 01398 323335
e-mail: info@exmoorsociety.com   Website: www.exmoorsociety.com
Office hours: Weekdays 10am to 4pm - Answerphone at all other times.

EDITORIAL

A warm welcome in this, the sixtieth year of Exmoor's designation as a National Park, to another Review with we hope something for everyone. For, as we are reminded at all our events and meetings, our readers come from many walks of life, with a huge variety of backgrounds and interests, not to mention contrasting points of view and priorities.

Within these pages you may read about Exmoor's birds and ponies, including a world champion. For many, Exmoor represents happy family holidays of yesteryear – read and smile at the childhood memory of being smothered in Mrs. Burge's bosom of clotted cream consistency – while for others Exmoor is a place of work, where serious conflicts between competing interests call for resolution – 'The Great Debate'.

Two beautifully illustrated interviews feature special people who have each made important contributions, both helping others to enjoy Exmoor in their different ways. Brian Chugg's photographs and notes conjure up chillingly the deep winter of 1963. And the winning entries in our two poetry competitions offer unique insights into what it means to live on, or visit, Exmoor – be it walking the dog, picking wild fruit, imagining oneself as a deer, trudging across open moor or simply responding to the vast tranquillity. Our Obituaries too celebrate individuals, whose fascinating and exemplary lives could easily have filled the whole issue.

One theme this year grew from the lively debate the Society fostered with its conference on the trees and woodlands of Exmoor. In considering Exmoor's trees, we move from a global context to an example of specific woodland management, with some reflections on the wider benefits of forests. The Society is leading a partnership studying the potential for Exmoor's woodlands, to plan what needs to be done, as did the Exmoor Society commissioned *Moorlands at a Crossroad* report.

Sadly, I don't have the space to mention all the articles in store, except to say that we move from the intriguing story of a church organ, via the Simonsbath Festival, an unusual farm visit, a now eerily disappeared pub, out on to the Coast path and beyond, deep into our now famous dark skies. And if the coming winter threatens to be anything like '63, we've some interesting books for you to draw near to the fire with...

Inevitably then, we offer personal views from right across the spectrum. The Society does not necessarily agree with every declared opinion, but welcomes their expression and debate, and hopes that you personally will find things both to agree with, and others perhaps to get you going, so to speak. For although we are many and different, there is at least one thing we all share, which binds us and justifies our Society – a love of Exmoor.

If you have a photograph or a written article that you would like considered for inclusion in the 2015 Review or on the Society's website, please contact me – we welcome contributions and your participation.

Richard Westcott

15

The Exmoor Society –
Christmas Cards for Sale

'A Winter's Day on Exmoor'
from a drawing by
Hope L Bourne 7" x 5"
in packs of 10 @ £5
plus p&p – see separate
order form.

CONTENTS

Cover picture: *Above Myrtleberry Cleave*, Jenny Gibson
Volume No. 55 ISBN 978 0 900131 77 6
© The Exmoor Society
Produced for the Exmoor Society by Halsgrove, Wellington, Somerset. Printed by Charlesworth Press

EXMOOR IN THE WINTER OF '63

Brian Chugg's text and photographs selected by Jenny Gibson

Brian Chugg (1926-2003) and his wife Mary were founder members of the Exmoor Society. Brian was known to readers of *The Guardian* as a 'Country Diary' writer, contributing once a fortnight for twenty-three years, often writing about Exmoor. For twenty-seven years he taught Art at the North Devon College of Further Education. There is an article on Mary elsewhere in this Review. The following are excerpts from Brian's field notebooks, accompanied by photographs he took at the time.

12 January 1963

Up lane to Shoulsbarrow - filled by deep drifts. Frozen hard enough to walk on but weak where twigs and grasses just underneath. Fox's footprints in evidence. Earthworks obliterated by snow. Crossed to triangulation point. Helicopters busy near Setta barrow. One landed near ponies? Followed hedge to Sloley Stone. Saw fox at 300 yds range. Deep drifts and cracking under my weight but not under foxes', which were much in evidence. Followed County

Near Moles Chamber.

Boundary to Edgerley Stone. Low cloud and light snow. Fox crossed my path at 75 yds range. Difficult walking. Snow soft and almost a foot deep in the open. Road from Edgerley Stone to Breakneck Hole under 8 to 10 ft. drifts. Lunch in quarry. Air full of minute ice needles. Frozen air?? At Challacombe snow plough had cleared about a mile from village. Walked up main road to Friendship Farm. Fields full of sheep. Road

Clearing snow between Friendship and Four Cross Way.

Near Five Cross Way.

cleared to Friendship and from there to point ¾ mile on way to 4 Cross Way. Then deep drifts not cleared for ¾ mile. Laundry van buried. Lift home from 4 Cross Way.

26 January 1963
From Breakneck Hole. Walking difficult in open. Deep drifts by hedges frozen. Possible to walk on this surface. Fox marks. Easy to keep warm today, 3 pullovers plus anorak. Pinkery obscured by deep drifts, water seepage under dam but outlet frozen. Grouse. Visibility very varied. Vixen? barked. Walked east towards Long Chains Combe in dense mist (thaw coming). Sun obscured. Had to take compass direction. Walking v. difficult in foot deep snow and lonely. Eventually came to valley only recognised after some time as Long Chains Combe by the 3 trees on the south side. The stream frozen completely in upper reaches, partially all the way down, but its bed provided best going.

Hoaroak Valley; impressed by absolute whiteness of everything. Going still difficult.

1 pm Trees below Hoaroak Cottage. Saw single sheep on side of Hoaroak Hill. Just as I was finishing lunch heard human voices to my surprise. Two shepherds on horse back, carrying hay with 3 dogs appeared. They had been feeding 500 sheep in Farley Water so brought hay for ponies. Helped them to round up half

dozen. Shepherds had come from Brendon Common – very difficult, they said.

South Furzehill. Sheep marooned in drifts provided dinner for foxes. Very deep drifts, the size of bungalows.

Barbrook only just in time to catch only bus back!

"The snow and ice had a distinctly mountainous appearance today particularly in the dense vaporous mist which, when it lifted, produced many mysterious and subtle effects of each merging

Lane near South Furzehill.

with the sky. There were moments of great clarity and visibility extended to as much as 3 miles. Edges and depressions in the snow field were given intensity. At other times one saw only the billowing snow forms: a cornice over an erosion channel or the frozen lines of a stream. The great white emptiness seemed purifying."

16 Feb. 1963

10.30 a.m. High Gate, Brendon. It had thawed for 2 days but heavy frost from the start. Mr Burgess of Lynmouth unable to take me beyond this point. Road blocked by deep drifts. Visibility at its lowest. Sky very dark. At beginning of Middle Hill – Farley Water Combe, great snow drift and ice sheet with overhanging cornice several feet thick. Road covered in thick ice where surface clear. Singer "Gazelle" abandoned between this point and Brendon Two Gates.

11.45. Brendon Two gates. Via Farley Water Visibility 50 yds. Road blocked ahead. A scene of absolute negation as though one had come face to face with death. 12.30 p.m. Hoaroak Tree. Drifts had thawed and were now frozen solid. Difficulty walking on steep inclines Much snow.

1.30 pm Lunch. Nr. Hoaroak Cottage. Sheep seen – not emaciated, made off when I arrived. Frost over 1 inch thick on thorn.

2 pm Hoaroak cottage Visibility slightly better

3pm Roborough Great snow cornice on west slope of Hoaroak Water drop looked about 10 ft and ¾ mile in length.

3.50 pm Arrived Barbrook.

Great snow cornice – Middle Badgworthy.

19

23 February

Brendon Two Gates 10 15 am. Road ploughed just to this point. Heavy frost, visibility 300yds.

11.30 am. Junction Hoccombe - Buscombe Large snow and ice fields. Drifts had thawed and frozen again. Very firm and slippery on slopes. Watched 2 foxes on opposite hillside marauding for food. One eventually sat down and appeared to watch me. Dropped glove etc. and had to climb down ice slope to retrieve them, difficult going, spread-eagled once or twice.

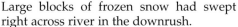

12 pm. Trout Hill. Snow cornice visible on east side of upper reaches of Badgworthy Deep drifts.

1 pm. East of Badgworthy inspected massive snow cornice, walked along upper edge. Hillside again very slippery. Difficult going. Finished last part on my back, but ankle not twisted! Avalanches from cornice had sheared off hawthorn trunks 7 inches thick near ground. Whole hillside had been scraped and was one solid mass of ice.

Large blocks of frozen snow had swept right across river in the downrush.

1.45 Badgworthy. Lunch. Walked down west side to Lank Combe Junction. Then thro Badgworthy woods. Saw fox at about 60 yds. Looked at each other for several minutes. Eventually I barked at it, but it continued looking. Climbing thro wood I found dead sheep with cheeks and eyes eaten. Fox feeding.

3 pm. Great Black Hill. The moor looks very white from this vantage point, areas near Dunkery particularly so. On western finger of moor only about 10% of land surface was covered.

Malmsmead Hill on to Brendon - Oare road.

4 pm. Brendon. Took road up to main A39. On way up a herd of wild ponies trotted frightened down the road followed by 2 shepherds in Army great coats. One wearing pebble lenses, looked as though he could see about 2 feet. A.39 still under inches of ice and deeply rutted

5.30 Lynmouth. Cold wind again now.

CRYING THE MOOR

An Exmoor Miscellany

BBC Countryfile comes to Exmoor

In January 2013 BBC Countryfile devoted much of a programme to Exmoor. Presenter Matt Baker went on a quest to discover how much of R. D. Blackmore's novel *Lorna Doone* is fiction and how much is fact. Riding in a landau from Malmsmead to Oare Church with Exmoor Society member and walk leader Jenny Gibson, they talked about how the novel originally became a success. At Oare he met Rev. Colin Burke, who gave some of the background to the famous wedding scene. And even-

TONY GIBSON

Matt Baker and Jenny Gibson.

tually he took a hair-raising Landrover trip with Rob Wilson-North, ENPA Conservation Manager, and land agent Ben Williams, from Dry Bridges to the deserted Mediaeval Village, which R. D. Blackmore probably had in mind when he created Glen Doone, stronghold of the famous outlaws.

COURTESY OF THE BBC

Jessy Emery (Somerset Wildlife Trust) and Julia Bradbury with children from Cutcombe School examing barn owl pellets.

Meanwhile, Julia Bradbury joined children from Cutcombe and Timberscombe schools, when they met Breeze the barn owl. An excerpt from Cutcombe School newsletter says: 'Congratulations to all the children, including the Eco Club from Timberscombe, who were really patient and exceptionally well-behaved – they managed to sit still and quiet for a 20 minute stretch of filming.'

At the same time, the Countryfile film crew also visited Dulverton Middle school where they made a film about the Exmoor Curriculum, filming some the pupils at work cutting down holly

21

trees in Burridge Woods. But lack of time meant that this episode was not broadcast until April. Dave Gurnett, Education Manager at ENPA, who was also interviewed in the programme, says: 'The children were very excited and really wanted Adam Henson to be the interviewer because he has respect as a farmer with these youngsters. That said, Jules Hudson was very interested in the holly clearance task and great fun was had by all. Since the filming enquiries have come from organisations in other National Parks that are keen to replicate the model. It would seem that "we" have lit a fire, because the interest is definitely there.'

Julia Bradbury also went on the trail of photographer Alfred Vowles, who left such a huge photographic record of life on Exmoor during the first half of the 20th century. First she met Margaret Jordan, whose account of Vowles's early life follows below; then with the help of the Minehead Harriers and Minehead photographer Ray Turner, she set about recreating a Vowles picture of a hunt meet at Hindon Farm, near Selworthy.

From Parish Records to Countryfile

I began researching the history of the village in which I live some twenty five years ago. This small village within the parish of Compton Bishop was once a busy coaching stop, with three inns to serve the trade, on the then Bristol to Bridgwater Turnpike road. As the story unfolded I became interested in the lives of the people who lived and worked in the parish. Their story often begins with a baptism in the parish church. From there I was able to collect outline family trees and found that many families had been there for many generations though sadly few now remained.

One such family was that of Vowles, true Somerset farming stock. Purely by chance I met someone researching their own line of the Vowles family and she told me that a member of the family had become a photographer on Exmoor. This discovery led to a fascinating story of a man whose love of the countryside and later Exmoor left us with a wealth of photographs and writing between 1910 and c1947.

Alfred Vowles (he styled himself as AV) was born in 1882. When he was only three years old his father died and the family were left in straitened circumstances. Despite this, in adult life, he described having a loving and happy childhood. A family friend and distant relative Charles Fry got AV a job with Eastman Kodak in London. This was to lead to travels with the accountant to Berlin and later Moscow and St. Petersburg. AV borrowed a camera and took photographs on his travels, sometimes in places where the taking of photographs was strictly forbidden!

When he returned to England he left London to return to country life and began to use his photographs to give lectures and lantern slide shows. Needing an income he got a job as an assistant photographer and began travelling miles, firstly on a bike, later a motor bike, around the countryside. He eventually settled on Exmoor living and working for many years in a horse drawn caravan.

I was surprised last year to be contacted by a researcher from the BBC Countryfile television series; I never did get a chance to discover how they found me. Despite some of the worst weather I have ever encountered on Exmoor it was interesting to see how the programme was put together. The whole team were very supportive as the moment for being 'on camera' arrived. From a faded entry in Compton Bishop parish register to Countryfile – and from that programme I hope many more people will appreciate the legacy AV left to the people of Exmoor.

Phytophthora Ramorum

One of the saddest events in the national park during 2011/2012 was the appearance of the fungal like pathogen *Phytophthora ramorum* which started to kill the extensive stands of Japanese Larch, particularly those in the North Eastern corner of the park. To counteract this the Forestry Commission issued Statutory Felling Orders to the landowners, including the National Trust, Crown Estates, the ENP and a number of private estates, in order to try and contain the spread of the disease.

The beautiful Comberow Valley, below Raleghs Cross, was particularly hard hit by the felling as the Larch, which covered much of the south face of the valley, was by then reaching maturity. The resultant exposure and devastation of the valley side will be visible for several years until the replanting of more resilient softwoods, which has already taken place, matures. Unfortunately, during the felling it was necessary to cut access tracks across the steep hillsides to allow mechanised forestry equipment to remove the timber, and this, combined with its foliage being stripped and retained on site to prevent further spreading of the disease, has added to the look of barrenness and to soil erosion.

After tree felling in Comberow Valley.

JUDY MOSS

Fortunately, one good outcome of the exposure of this land is the flowering of ranks of foxgloves, ferns and other plants that until now have lain dormant under the shadows of the trees. And the valley is much lighter now.

However, despite the precautions taken, many thousand of hectares of Larch across South Wales, the north-west of England and the south-west of Scotland are being affected by this unnatural disaster. Plus we have yet to see the impact of Sudden Ash Death across the country. All in all a very depressing prospect.

Felling larch in the Comberow Valley.

However, if you live in a managed forest, change is inevitable.

Joint walks with the Dartmoor Preservation Association

2013 has been the third year of the joint walks with the DPA. Sadly, fewer Exmoor Society members make the journey to Dartmoor than DPA members visiting Exmoor, but all the walks have been generally well-attended and blessed with reasonable, if not perfect, weather. A great deal of thought is put into choosing the theme and itinerary for the walks, to show each other special aspects of our respective moors. The DPA tend to focus on sites of archaeological interest, of which Dartmoor has such a wealth; for instance, the remains of over 5,000 Bronze Age roundhouses, and some spectacular

Exmoor Society and DPA members near Doone Valley.

stone rows. Our 2013 trip included a visit to Higher Uppacott, a Grade 1 listed long-house, with the shippon unchanged since it was built.

We on Exmoor have shown our Dartmoor colleagues red deer during the rut in 2011, with a record number of 40 walkers; the Doone Valley in 2012; and in 2013 we will be walking through former Acland country from Selworthy to where Exmoor meets the sea at Hurlstone Point. These walks have helped to highlight the fact that the two moors, although so close geographically, have very different flora and fauna, geology and history.

The Devon and Somerset Pony Club

The Pony Club is one of the largest inter-national equestrian youth organisations, with almost 100,000 members, run by volunteers for children up to the age of 20 (or 25 years for associate members). There are around 350 clubs (and some centres providing ponies) which cover designated 'areas' across the UK. The Exmoor National Park is home to the Devon and Somerset Pony Club (D&S PC) which currently has around 90 members.

The D&S PC offer mounted and un-mounted rallies throughout the year as well as a variety of events and competi-tions. There are teams in most disciplines, as well as sponsored rides, training shows and fun days. Members are also encour-aged to progress through ability levels which start from the basic 'E' test through to H and ultimately A, the highest level.

Pony Club member Katie Hanson on Arthur.

Warmer weather (hopefully) signals the first of two annual 'camps' held for three and four days respectively, for juniors and seniors. Juniors as well as improving their riding skills, learn how to care for their pony with a fun competition held on the last day. Senior camp which is residential, often sees around forty combinations enjoy a week of looking after their own horse, riding, training, competing – and not forgetting the legendary water fighting!

Three interesting facts about the Pony Club:
• Each of the winning 2012 British Olympic Event Team members came through the Pony Club.
• The Pony Club's vision is to 'promote the highest ideals of sportsmanship, citizenship and loyalty to create strength of character and self-discipline, health and well-being'.

- The D&S PC has been described as 'a large family where life-long friendships are made'.

If you would like to know more, contact details for the D&S PC are:
Sue McCanlis (Chairman) sue.voyager@hotmail.co.uk.
The D&S PC website: http://devonandsomersetponyclub.blogspot.com

Young Farmers Club (YFC)

The first Young Farmers Club began in 1921 in Hemyock, Devon. Other clubs soon sprang up providing social as well as educational opportunities. Today the NFYFC (National Federation of Young Farmers Clubs) has over 700 clubs nationally and 23,000 members. Somerset alone has 24 clubs which make up five groups, representing each corner of the county. Ages vary from 10 to 26 years and you don't need to 'be one to be one'.

Exmoor is home to several clubs (please see website for your nearest). Each one runs its own programme of events for the year which is decided by the members. In addition to this there are County sports and competitions throughout the year, the winners of which can go to an Area play-off and finally to the National Finals, run by the National Federation of Young Farmers' Clubs based in Warwickshire. There are also Public Speaking events, Drama, Pantomime and Entertainments finals, the County Ball, Three Counties Ball, sports, Stock Judging and so much more. Also members make friends throughout Somerset, as well as regionally, nationally or through International Exchange, internationally. Activities cover the whole age spectrum, with the junior members supervised during activities and camps.

Junior YFC Wiveliscombe member Frank Normal winning his section with sheep.

Young Farmers Clubs are run by the members (each club has advisory support and club leaders) for the members. County office offers support as well as ensuring that Child Protection policies, Health and Safety risk assessments etc are carried out to minimise any risk involved.

If you would like more information or to find out where your nearest club is, please ring 01278 691711 and speak to Gillian (Office Manager, membership and finance officer), Katherine (full-time administrator) or Anna (part-time administrator) or contact the office via e-mail: admin@somersetyfc.org.uk or websites: Somersetyfc.org.uk or devonyfc.co.uk

Storm Damage in the National Park

The ENPA maintains 991 km (615miles) of public rights of way. We supply and fit the majority of gates and stiles, and maintain all the signing, bridges and surfaces. Between April 2012 and March 2013 we carried out the following works:

Kilometres of paring	**103.24**
M^2 of path regrading	**146.40**
Number of drains maintained	**435**
Number of windblown trees cleared	**838**
Number of hazardous trees cleared	**74**
Number of signs	**456**
Number of sign posts	**206**
Number of field gates	**134**
Number of new bridge sections	**15**

The floods in Dec 2012 followed by the heavy snow caused a huge amount of damage. Five bridges suffered significant damage, one of which (Horsen footbridge) was washed away completely. Many river side paths have suffered severe surface damage, especially along the Barle. There were two major landslips along the coast at Greenaleigh and Crock Pits. Large number of inland tracks have been washed out or gullied.

In response to this we have done the following: 670 trees were cleared in the first quarter of this year (80% of our usual annual total). Three bridges were repaired or rebuilt. The two remaining (Horsen and Cornham) are major operations, that will be done later this year. We have also carried out a huge amount of resurfacing work and drain construction. 244km (152 miles) of paths were walked by people with saws to clear fallen trees and branches.

TIM PARISH

Horsen Ford with Cow Castle in the background.

Dark Skies

"For thousands of years, man has looked upwards at the night sky and wondered at what he saw. The wonder helped to define our sense of who we are, our myths and legends, our religious beliefs and our sense of our place in a wider cosmos. But the dark skies that were the night time backdrop for the vast majority of human history are for many of us now a rare sight. Our night times are filled with the orange glow of street lighting and we are all more likely to be looking at the television than looking at the stars." – ENPA Dark Skies Guide.

Incredible though it may seem to us on Exmoor who are used to looking out into a dark (if frequently cloudy) night sky, it comes as a shock to realise that we are among only 5 per cent of the population of this country to enjoy truly dark skies and that more than half live with severe light pollution.

Now National Park Centres in Dunster, Dulverton and Lynmouth are able to offer high performance telescopes for hire allowing people to explore Exmoor's stunning dark starry skies, although International Dark Sky Week from 5 -11 April 2013 turned into a rather cloudy event. Exmoor National Park was designated Europe's first International Dark Sky Reserve in 2011. Since then, so called 'astrotourism' has grown in popularity, with a number of local businesses offering stargazing breaks and stargazing safaris.

Telescopes can be hired for £25 per night (plus a refundable deposit). They are easy to transport and use and are suitable for all the family and come complete with instructions and a guide on how to find different night sky features depending on the time of the year. The telescopes are also ideal for groups who may be looking for something different to do during their visit. For further information and to book a telescope, please contact any of the National Park Centres.

Tarr Steps

On 23rd December 2012, Exmoor experienced its worst flooding for many years. People were forced to leave their homes, property was damaged and there was considerable local disruption. The River Barle rose swiftly and dramatically reaching levels close to those of the catastrophic flood of August 1952. People who witnessed the flood were struck by the amount of water in the river, but more disturbing was its immense velocity. The river tore healthy trees from its banks and once in the floodwaters they became projectiles hurled against any obstacles in their path.

It was not surprising therefore that, during the flood, a number of historic bridges were badly affected. Tarr Steps – the 'ancient' 17 span, clapper bridge across the Barle between Hawkridge and Winsford – was severely damaged. Many of the clapper stones which form the walkway were displaced and one, weighing as much as 2 tonnes, was carried 20 metres downstream.

Tarr Steps is the responsibility of Somerset County Council, and repair work was arranged in a very timely fashion with full consultation over the sensitivities of both the structure itself (which is a Scheduled Monument) and with those responsible for the management of the adjacent land (including a National Nature Reserve). Before repairs could begin, however, Exmoor was gripped by heavy snows, which further weakened some riverside trees and snapped massive branches off others. As the snow thawed the river rose again with meltwater. Once more trees and branches were carried down the river causing further damage. Eventually the conditions were stable enough to carry out the repairs to the Steps, and, watched on by national media, Tarr Steps was finally returned to its original state.

But how 'original' is original? It seems that Tarr Steps has been reconstructed regularly over the years and close scrutiny of old photographs shows how its form has subtly changed. In 2013 it took 4 or 5 people and a mechanical digger around 5 days to complete the task. Apparently in 1952 it took the army 30 men and 5 weeks to do the same. This raises the question of how such a structure could have been regularly repaired in the past without a considerable investment of time and labour. Did it not wash away so regularly...or is it not that old? It seemed as if the more we thought about Tarr Steps, the less explicable it became!

With that in mind Exmoor National Park has commissioned a study of Tarr Steps. Incredibly, this has never been done. The results are expected later on this year.

Vital statistics

In June 2013 it was announced that Exmoor has 1,327,200 tourist visits annually, with a spend of about £93 million, whereas Dartmoor has 2,276,000 visits spending about £119 million. Exmoor is 72% the size of Dartmoor. Extrapolated, this means that each visitor spends an average 70p on Exmoor, compared to 52p on Dartmoor. However, we only have 36% the total number of visitors.

©ENPA, TAKEN BY STEVE GUSCOTT

Rebuilding Tarr Steps.

Special thanks to Margaret Jordan for her contribution on Alfred Vowles, to Peter Moss on Phytophthora in the Comberow Valley, Cindy Cowling on the Pony Club and YFC, Tim Parish, ENPA Ranger, on flood damage and Rob Wilson-North, Conservation Manager ENPA, on Tarr Steps.

VALUING OUR NATIONAL PARKS

Rachel Thomas – Chairman of the Exmoor Society

In a period of economic downturn, landscape beauty is thought by some to be an outdated concept and growth is the only thing that matters. But such periods are precisely the wrong time to throw away the things we value, for these can provide a deeper source of pleasure and inner contentment than money can buy. Our national parks were specially selected in the twentieth century because they provided country-side that was semi-natural, semi-wild and open, and where traditional farming systems remained and rural communities were closely tied to the land and the seasons in their way of life. Although much has changed in the last sixty years, Exmoor and other national parks are still in essence places of scenic beauty, tranquillity and rurality that have been lost in many parts of the countryside.

England's ten national parks are valued nationally because of the wealth of natural assets found within them, a wealth that has increased since they were first designated, as new public benefits are discovered that enrich people's quality of life. In today's context, however, with the national debate over government spending on public services, it is right to provide evidence of how national parks contribute to the nation's prosperity and well-being, and how national parks are responding to the priority for growth, even though some of the benefits of the designation are priceless.

Five years ago in the *Exmoor Review*, volume 49, in an article titled 'Natural Beauty and Jobs and Prosperity', I wrote the following: 'There has long been the accusation that conservation is only concerned with preservation and not with livelihoods. Further, it has been argued that National Park designation in particular has had a negative impact on jobs and investment within their areas. So, it may come as a surprise to many people that some conservationists over the last few decades have searched for ways of inte-grating protection of the landscape with economic well-being and of realising the aim that designation can create new opportunities for wealth creation.' The article refers in more detail to two reports providing evidence that national park status is a positive economic benefit. It is particularly pleasing and timely then that National Park Authorities (NPAs) have now commissioned a report called *Valuing England's National Parks*, which shows the latest economic and socio-economic data from them, in order to assess their contribution to economic prosperity and well-being and identifying poten-tial opportunities to increase it.

It is an important contribution to the austerity debate to show that economic growth comes from protecting natural beauty and natural assets. The report shows that national park economies make a valuable contribution locally and nationally; that NPAs play an important role; and that although their economies face a range of challenges and oppor-tunities, the NPAs are uniquely placed to support future economic growth. Some of the data in the report shows the following characteristics and allows Exmoor to be compared with other national parks.

Population and Age Profile National parks jointly cover an area of more that 1.2 million hectares (ha) which is 9% of England's land area. Exmoor however is the third smallest national park with a land area of 69,000 ha. 321,000 people live in national parks, but Exmoor has a relatively small population of just over 10,000 people. The sparse population of national parks is indicated by their average population density of 0.3 persons per ha, with Exmoor's being 0.15 persons per ha which is the third lowest of all national parks. The population is older and population growth over the past 10 years has been lower in national parks than in England. Even compared with just the national parks' average of 33%, Exmoor has a larger population of over 60s at 39%. More surprisingly, Exmoor is the only national park where the population has declined between 2001 and 2011, and by 5.5%.

Economic Activity Of the working population, 70% is economically active in all national parks, but for Exmoor it is slightly lower at 67% which equates to approximately 7,600 people. National parks have a higher proportion of self employed people at 32% than England and a lower proportion of full time workers. The proportion of full time employees is particularly low on Exmoor at 24%, while self employment is particularly high at 26% compared even to other national parks at 19%. Unemployment is low for all national parks at 2%. Within them, there is a higher proportion of senior, professional and skilled occupations in the workforce and on Exmoor this accounts for 40% of all occupations, compared to national park averages of 32%. Average household incomes for most national parks are higher than regional averages, but for Exmoor at £28,668 it is the lowest of all national parks and significantly lower than the average household income for the South West region. House prices in all national parks command a significant premium compared with those in their regions and Exmoor was the third highest of all national parks.

Businesses and Gross Value Added (GVA) There are 22,500 businesses located in national parks providing around 141,000 jobs, but most are of a small size with under 10 employees. Data suggests that Exmoor has 830 businesses which have decreased by 6% since 2009, and 95% of the businesses have fewer than 10 employees which is higher than in other national parks. Key sectors in national park economies, not surprisingly, are farming and forestry which are responsible for managing the vast majority of national park areas and account for 39% of businesses on Exmoor compared with 24% for all national parks. Tourism and recreation attract 91 million visitors per annum jointly in national parks, with an annual visitor expenditure equating to £3 billion. However, it is noticeable that Exmoor only receives 1,334,500 visits, the lowest of all national parks and, with an estimated tourism expenditure of £89 million, the second lowest. There is a particularly strong focus on agriculture and tourism accounting, on Exmoor, for more than half the businesses which is significantly higher than across other national parks. Approximately 40% of Exmoor's turnover of £164 million comes from these two sectors. It is estimated that national parks generate between £4.1 billion to £6.3 billion GVA (depending on which data set is used) equivalent to a small city like Plymouth or the UK aerospace industry.

The report goes on to show that NPAs themselves play an important role in supporting their local economies as they have a direct impact in terms of employment and expenditure on goods and services. In 2011/12 gross expenditure across the parks amounted to £74m with £4.786m on Exmoor. This expenditure was funded through a grant from central government of £54m to the parks with Exmoor receiving £3.765m. The total public grant is equivalent to around £1 per annum per person in England. With the squeeze on public spending the total grant is to be reduced to £46.6m by 2014/15, which will obviously affect the level of services NPAs provide and the wider influence they can have on facing the challenges and opportunities in growing the economy, not least in the land-based sectors (farming, forestry, tourism, recreation and food) and partnership working on many projects and initiatives.

Matthew Parris in one of his weekly columns in *The Times* wrote that NPAs were right to fear cuts to their core funding as ministers would look for easy ones: 'I would cut something that confers a modest benefit on millions but a big gain on almost nobody - a service with no shrouds or bleeding stumps to wave.' He believes that the threat is not one of being abolished or sold off but of having 10% of income shaved off year after year and he urges us not to let the degradation of parks happen by stealth.

There is, therefore, an imperative on all of us in the national park movement to use every opportunity to publicise the importance of the designation and show that this can in fact create wealth. That is why the Exmoor Society has taken up the cause of supporting the ecosystem approach (see the article 'Where there is no vision' in the *Exmoor Review*, volume 53), for it shows the range of services provided and how they are valued by society and contribute to wider well-being. Some of these services are paid for by market mechanisms; others are more difficult to value or are being provided freely by those delivering them, particularly by farmers who manage most. Indeed, what price can be put on a view from Dunkery Beacon, hearing the skylarks, seeing red deer, experiencing wild country connecting with the wildness within us, or solitude and inner peace? – all benefits that are the result of the way the land is managed.

The government in the 2011 Natural Environment White Paper stated that there are real opportunities for land managers to gain by protecting nature's services and used the example of how a water company might pay a farmer for protecting the uplands so that they can clean and filter the water naturally. The Mires Project on Exmoor provides a practical case study where South West Water (SWW) is financing the blocking up of drainage ditches in order to rewet the peat. SWW can only extract water from the River Exe by licence which depends on the flow levels. Wimbleball Reservoir balances out flow through the year by pumping water into it at a pumping station at Exbridge. Savings can be made by the water company if pumping costs and treatment costs are reduced and if water can be retained for longer in the peat and released slowly so that flow levels are not so low in summer. So far, considerable funding by SWW has been put into drainage blocking and research work, particularly relating to the collection of data to monitor the hydrological impacts of drain blocking, archaeological findings, vegetation changes, breeding waders and invertebrate numbers. Farmers who have permitted SWW to rewet their land face extra costs and changes to their farming systems with only small financial recompense from Natural England through H.L.S. payments for biodiversity and rewetting. The challenge is to work out financial payments to the farmer from SWW for managing the quality and quantity of water from the peat moorland parts of their farm. For Exmoor, Payment for Ecosystems Services (PES) is an important step forward in finding ways to reward farmers for the many public benefits they provide. These wider services can contribute to making a livelihood from the land under their control where farming is handicapped by natural and other environmental constraints and diversification opportunities are limited.

Valuing England's National Parks is a timely reminder that national park designation has the potential to help economic growth and prosperity and general well-being. The NPAs play a key role particularly when they concentrate on protecting and enhancing natural capital. However, there is a danger that they are being overstretched to deliver other services and are becoming more like the old Rural District Councils, forgetting that local authorities still provide their functions and services within the national park areas. NPAs cannot solve all the challenges facing the economies of their areas. Considering that protecting and enhancing natural capital is the NPA's core business, it is surprising that spending in key activities does not reflect this. Total gross expenditure for all NPAs is as follows: conservation of natural environment and cultural heritage (20%), recreation, management and transport, promoting understanding, rangers, estates and volunteers (40%), development management, forward planning and communities (28%), corporate and democratic core (12%).

The Exmoor Society has argued that the ENPA could alter the balance of its spending to the conservation section with less on administering the membership and planning and communities section and more on stimulating farming and tourism. The one thing that is lacking to my mind is a deeper understanding and knowledge of farming economics and the running of an agricultural business and land management practices. These aspects are fundamental when deciding on practical agri-environmental schemes that will work on Exmoor where local conditions and knowledge are different from other national parks. The ENPA has developed considerable skills and knowledge in its conservation section and land based projects, and this is where its financial priorities should lie. It is pleasing to note that it has listened to our concerns and is making a new staff appointment to take forward the eco-system approach, which of course involves farming businesses.

It is also up to the wider national park movement and charities like the ES to take up the challenge of defending these special areas and not shy away from helping develop their economies with the need for a fairer financial return to managers of the land. At the same time, there is a requirement to continually publicise the wider benefits provided by natural beauty and enjoyment so that we can work towards the government and NPAs' 2030 vision: 'The national parks will be recognised as fundamental to our prosperity and wellbeing'.

ᴜLES CHAMBER – AN ENIGMATIC PLACE

Peter Pay

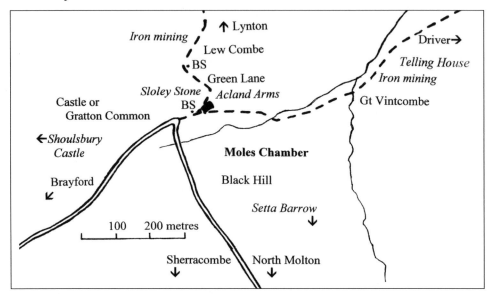

I am gazing into the dramatic ravine of Great Vintcombe from a scenic ridge above the Barle Valley. Although the ground here only dips a little below the summit, there is a surprising amount of water running noisily into foreboding marshes. This area is a watershed. A tributary of the Barle starts here and, over there on the other flank of the ridge, streams feed into the Bray. It is said that in 1852 Reverend Mole came through here on horseback and vanished into one of these bogs, which is why this forlorn place is called Moles Chamber.

At my feet there is a short section of moss-covered stonewall. This footing, and a few scattered stones, is all that remains of the Acland Arms tavern, once situated at the junction of four tracks. In 1852, I could have entered the pub and taken a pot of ale with *patchers*, the surface miners, who rootle for minerals in the ground near here. George Chapple, the innkeeper is out today tending his sheep on enclosures leased from Thomas Acland of Little Bray. The publican's wife, Charlotte, explains that this place has always been known as Moles Chamber. She also recalls the story of a drunken farmer riding from South Molton, losing his way in the dark and perishing in the mire below.

A little research soon reveals that the 1651 Survey of Exmoor marks this place Moales Chamber. The 1841 Census lists Moles Chamber as an 'Extra Parochial Place of Exmoor' and in 1851 the Census refers to Moules Chamber. Whatever equestrian shortcomings the Revd Mole experienced in 1852, lending his moniker to this corner of Exmoor happened too late to be a credible explanation for the name.

The source of the River Mole is five miles away at Darlick Moor, probably too far to explain a connection. Perhaps the ancient Celtic name *Moel*, a bald hill, is relevant. Is 'Chamber' an archaic word indicating an enclosed space, holding pens, or does it indicate a hollow in this terrain, a cave, a drover's refuge, or an ancient burial site on the bald hill? Ancient history abounds around here and it is likely that place names are as old as the monuments nearby. The impressive Iron Age hill-fort called Shoulsbury Castle with its Bronze Age barrow is less than a mile away, as is Setta Barrow.

Roman history is also relevant. Nearby excavations have recently revealed a Romano-British and medieval iron-smelting site at Sherracombe, only 1.7 miles distant below the ridge. *Moll*, possibly a word of Irish origin, means heaped land. There is no obvious evidence of an ancient burial site at Moles Chamber but there is hillocky ground to be found nearby. I wandered down the picturesque, green-lane only a few hundred paces to Lew Combe to see the upheaval caused by surface workings there. Rusty stains seep from piles of disturbed ground and suspiciously heavy stones show traces of iron ore.

The 'green lane' to Lew Combe is really only one prominent bank capped with a beech hedge. There is a path either side of this bank and the lane running back to Moles Chamber probably occupies a boundary ditch – a 'scratch' lane. The eye-catching Sloley Stone, dated 1742, marked a boundary here. To the west, Castle Common, once called Gratton Common, includes the Shoulsbury Iron Age hill-fort. The stone proclaims that this was the domain of 'Christian Slowley, Lady of the Manor of Gratton'. To the east the land belonged to 'William Oxenham, Lord of the Manor of High Bray'. Other boundary markers, 'mearestones', can be found, like the Hore Stone at Lew Combe partially buried, its inscription illegible.

Next I take the other track into the Barle Valley towards Driver, on the so-called Hare Path that led to Simonsbath and Exe Head. Again, at the junction of two cleaves, there is evidence of surface mining. Above this spot, on the promontory, is a circular mound. Little remains now but Roger Burton claims to have found here the site of a Telling House from where the annual sheep count was conducted through the eighteenth century. In the spring the fees for grazing sheep, cattle and 'horse beasts' on the moor was proclaimed in local market towns; a practice known as 'crying the moor'. Farmers gave notice of numbers of grazing animals and their brands, or 'stand marks', were entered into the 'Forest Book'. At strategic places, like Span Head and near Moles Chamber, tellers counted the animals entering the moor, the fifteenth of June traditionally being a day of general commotion.

Returning to the ridge road it is hardly possible to picture the Acland Arms in its heyday. About 1820 Daniel Bright rented land on Black Moor from Thomas Palmer Acland of Little Bray and built a dwelling nearby in Moles Chamber with 'two good-sized rooms and three chambers over'. A public house was first licensed by James Hewett in 1824. John Chick became the innkeeper in 1826 and when he died in 1834 his widow Charlotte soon remarried George Chapple. The 1841 Census lists two dwellings at Moles Chamber, one housing agricultural labourers, the other the publican George Chapple, his wife Charlotte and her children from the previous marriage. The 1851

Census records the inn housing George Chapple, his family and a lodger. The labourers' dwelling was by then uninhabited.

Charlotte's daughter Susannah helps in the pub and will soon be married to Jeremiah Smyth of Challacombe who seems to be a solid sort of chap. He was born in Simonsbath, the son of a gardener employed on John Knight's estate before the family moved to farm at Challacombe. Susannah and Jeremiah marry in 1858 at Simonsbath. In the 1861 Census they are living in Marwood parish, he described as a farm labourer and iron miner. Jeremiah was briefly the licensee of the Sportsman's Inn at Sandy Way and from 1863 they ran the Acland Arms.

The Acland Arms relied on a steady trade from the packhorse trains as it stood at the intersection of routes from Lynmouth, Simonsbath, Brayford and North Molton. There was brief prosperity when iron-ore prospecting in the 1850s brought an influx of miners seeking accommodation. Sadly the boom years were short lived and trade had faded by 1883 when the licence was discontinued. The publican, Jeremiah Smyth was by then more profitably engaged in farming 79 acres and tending stock for Thomas Acland. Twelve children were raised at Moles Chamber and by 1890 this large family had moved to farm at Natsley, in the Bray Valley below. The Acland Arms was abandoned and within ten years was uninhabitable. Frederick Snell in his *Book of Exmoor* reported that the walls and porch were still standing in 1903 whilst the garden was a ruin.

Moles Chamber is a forlorn spot and many visitors have reported sensing a strange atmosphere here. Most disconcerting is the absence of the dwellings and lost memories of the families that toiled in this harsh environment. The tracks, boundary stones and green lane remain, as does the mining spoil. The people are long departed and it is difficult to trace where the inn and its buildings were sited, or to be certain what the name Moles Chamber once signified.

Allen N. V., *Meanings and Derivations*, Alcombe Books, 1986
Burton R. A., *Heritage of Exmoor*, RAB, 1989
Burton R. A., *Simonsbath*, RAB, 1994
Burton S., *Exmoor*, Hodder & Stoughton, 1969
Eardley-Wilmot H., Pinkery and Driver, *Exmoor Review* vol 24, 1983, p50
MacDermot E. T., *History of the Forest of Exmoor* (1911), David & Charles, 1973
Orwin S. C., *Reclamation of Exmoor Forest* (1929), Exmoor Books, 1997
Riley & Wilson-North, *Field Archaeology of Exmoor*, English Heritage, 2001
Snell F. J., *Book of Exmoor* (1903), Halsgrove, 2002
Wilson-North R., Recording the iron mines of Exmoor, *PDMHS*, 1996, p137-142

I am grateful to Rob Wilson-North for guidance in historical research, Jessica Turner formerly of ENPA for maps and to Lionel Huxtable for information about his family and location of the Acland Arms pub.

Dr Peter Pay lectured in Fine Art studies, exhibits sculpture, is a self-directed student of historical geology, walker and amateur musician.

RICHARD ACLAND – HE HAD A GIFT

Douglas Stuckey

Sir Richard Acland electioneering when he contested the North Devon seat in 1945.

There are few names connected with Exmoor more fit to conjure with than the name of Acland, for from father to son, and heir to heir, they have handed on a tradition of benevolent altruism, of personal charm and broadminded piety, of good landlordism and a temper of politics which has suited the West Country people now for over three centuries gone by.

Thus Walter Joyce opened the 'Ole Zur Tummus' chapter in his *Moorland Tales and Talk* published in 1935. Perhaps a little deferential in tone, nevertheless the scale of Acland's influence and importance could hardly be overestimated … popular legend at one time averred that one could walk from the Bristol to the English Channel without leaving Acland land – not strictly accurate but the family owned land in contiguous parishes from one waterway to the other.

The Acland name is complicated. In 1155 Henry II gave land round Landkey to a Hugh de Accalen (probably a Flemish mercenary who had served the King) and the name hardened over time to Acland. The medieval farm of Acland Barton became a family home. In the early seventeenth century the family left Acland Barton for a larger home at Culm John, close to the present day Killerton. The Aclands grew and flourished not unassisted by a succession of fruitful marriages to wealthy heiresses. Sir Richard Acland, as part of his ethically driven disbursements in 1945, sold the Barton to its tenants.

Over the centuries the Aclands were prominent in agricultural improvement, parliamentary business, and hunting the red deer down the valley of the Barle; they were not naturally ostentatious, fitting easily into the role of first among equals but, of course, the class structure was very rigid and the great families were expected to maintain a style appropriate to their position. One young Acland recalled travelling regally:

'I remember the excitement of arriving by train at Exeter, where a footman would be waiting for us on the platform looking very smart with a cockade at the side of his top-hat. There was a carriage and pair outside and we were driven to Killerton with two large Dalmatians running behind the carriage. As we got near Killerton everyone recognised the carriage and the village men and boys all touched their hats, while the women and girls made little curtsies.'

The 1914–1918 war shook society to its foundations. The then Sir Charles Thomas Acland, usually known as Thomas, who died in 1919 and not considered a natural reformer, in his final years initiated the first of the changes which eventually secured Exmoor for the nation. In *The Times* of 22 February 1917 – an issue which carried a War Office list of 1,620 killed, wounded and taken prisoner – there appeared a letter from the Earl of Plymouth, Chairman of the Executive Committee of the National Trust:

'I hope you will allow us to announce through your columns a very interesting and important gift which has just been made to the National Trust ... the larger portion of the lands which come under this arrangement includes a great part of the valleys of Horner and Selworthy ... as well as the farm at Cloutsham ... the two smaller portions include the wilder parts of North Hill which runs down to Hurlstone and a stretch of the wild moorland of Winsford Hill. We believe that in agreeing to take what is the new departure and for the first time accept something less than ownership, the Trust is finding a new and useful way of discharging its duty to the nation.'

In the early twentieth century the Liberal Party flourished and the Acland family were among its foremost stalwarts, and Killerton a sort of Liberal centre. Lloyd George launched his famous Land Campaign addressing around 19,000 in the park of Killerton.

In June 1939 the then fourteenth baronet, Sir Francis Acland died and Richard succeeded as the fifteenth baronet. Richard Acland was born on the 26th November 1906, educated at Rugby school and Balliol and, at first, his life followed a busy and conventional path. Qualified as a barrister and architect, he served for a first time as a lieutenant in the 96th (Royal Devon Yeomanry) Field Brigade, Royal Artillery. He married Anne Alford, architect and designer, who proved an active and wise counsellor in the years that followed.

Richard stood for Parliament for the North Devon seat in 1935, and was returned. In a letter to this writer in 1983 he described entertainingly electioneering at that time:

'True enough North Devon elections were "rumbustious". But more so than today? Well yes, no doubt, because in those days the village meeting mattered because, with one candidate coming on Tuesday and the other on Friday, the talk in the village pub would be about two performances; whereas today what matters is that you don't miss the evening's TV. I often heard the tradition that a Liberal candidate had once been thrown over the quay at Appledore. But rumbustiousness never came to anything like that level in my day. My fiancé and I, in 1935, announced that we should speak at every village hall and hamlet (as well as in the few towns) in the last two days. It involved 72 meetings at times such as 10.17 and 3.51. Loudspeakers were then so new that people ran from their houses to see what was happening when our vehicle started up in the village centre just four minutes before Anne and I were due to arrive. We had a torchlight victory procession; but I believe North Devon Liberals still do.

In 1931 the Free Church influence was very important indeed. I hardly had one Anglican as a prominent supporter.'

At the time that Richard entered Parliament Europe was reeling after the most vicious recession and from the growth of Nazi and Fascist parties. The Aclands had been Tories and Liberals but they had a tendency to lean contrarily towards reform and even rebel causes; an Acland was the only Tory MP to argue in favour of the Reform Bill of 1852. Consequently, it was not surprising that events led Richard to become an ardent socialist.

He decided to put his principles into practice by forming a new political movement, Forward March, which certainly struck a chord with popular feelings in the 1940s. To answer Hitler's *Mein Kampf* (My Struggle) he wrote *Unser Kampf* (Our Struggle) which sold a remarkable 13,200 copies and guaranteed that his name appeared high on the list of those to be eliminated if Hitler won.

At that time, J.B. Priestley had formed a similar pressure group, the 1941 Committee. Acland and Priestley combined to form a new political party, Common Wealth, to break the wartime electoral truce. (Priestley, that brilliant, quirky Yorkshireman was not really designed for that dull slog of political activity and soon withdrew.) Common Wealth secured some remarkable electoral success winning three parliamentary seats, each candidate being a serving officer. Anxious to finance Common Wealth which was engaged in vigorous and costly publicity such as posters on the Underground – 'What is morally wrong cannot be economically or politically right' – he pondered selling his Exmoor estates but, persuaded by his wife Anne, he made the different and remarkable decision to give his ancient properties (approximately 18,000 acres) to the National Trust to hold in perpetuity for the nation. 'When I look out I do not want to say "this is mine" or "this is yours" but "this is ours".'

However with the Labour party landslide victory, a large proportion of CW members drifted into its ranks hoping to see its ideals realised under the new government.

Acland became for a time a Labour MP for Gravesend and served as a Second Church Commissioner from 1950 to 1951. He soon fell out with Labour, particularly over nuclear issues, spending some time as a teacher at Wandsworth Grammar School and returning westward became a senior lecturer at St Luke's College of Education in Exeter founded by his ancestors. He continued to write and publish abundantly 'like a disenchanted but still hopeful idealist'.

In 1964 he wrote a treatise on education called 'Curriculum of Life', in which he hoped that 'courageous teachers' would inspire the young to eschew the rampant materialism of the era, so that in 20 years' time ours would be a genuinely democratic and religious society.

When the great transfer of his lands took place, Acland prepared simultaneously a Memorandum of Wishes which he hoped would be honoured by the new custodians. Perhaps inevitably, in time, some differences arose. Not long before his death a vote at a National Trust AGM proposing a ban on stag hunting on its property aroused his ire. No hunter himself he had wished nevertheless to ensure that hunting along with other traditional customs and cultures of the moor be allowed to continue unaltered. His letter of protest to the Earl of Antrim at the National Trust was lucid, as usual, and coolly patrician:

'When I have made my complaints in the accepted way ... the result on each and every occasion has been a "cover up" operation by one officer or another resulting in a face-saving conclusion whereby no one appears to be blameworthy.'

Richard was proud of his honourable ancestry and that pride was fused with a determination to be a prophet for a better future. Of course, some found aspects of his political wisdom unconvincing but few doubted his integrity or could deny his personal charm. He pursued his contemporaries with an evangelical zeal, with sometimes as seemingly unlikely converts as Lady Astor and Mick Jagger.

In 1990 he spent several weeks in hospital suffering from heart problems, but returned home to Broadclyst determined to continue campaigning against the anti-stag hunting lobby. He died in Exeter on 24 November 1990 and the *Somerset County Gazette* reported: *'Elderly residents of the picture-postcard cottages of Selworthy were saddened to learn of the death of Sir Richard Acland... who is remembered locally as the last of a long line of benevolent squires.'*

Douglas Stuckey is of West Country ancestry, educated at Shebbear, served in 'Dad's Army' and the RNVR, and worked in industry and publishing. He and his wife Dora were members of the National Committee of Common Wealth for many years. He would like particularly to thank the National Trust for their help while he was researching and preparing this article.

MALMSMEAD

David Spark

A distinct memory, just before the war, was of standing with Mum, Dad and Brian outside Oare Church as darkness fell, and watching the lights of an Austin 10 winding down the road from County Gate. Uncles Jack and Herbert had driven from Hexham to join us, camping in a field at Oaremead. There were glow worms that night, and in the morning big fat black slugs. We bathed up at Weir Water and picked wortle-berries on our way back to our tents.

From a postcard in my collection:

Malmsmead 12 Sept.   *Postmark Brendon P SP 13 1909*
*   Do you remember this spot? We came here on the 8th, & have had bad weather so far. Went to meet of Staghounds at Brendon Two Gates yesterday – thick mist and much rain – no hunting. Foxhounds meet here tomorrow, & at Oareford on Wednesday, & Staghounds at Hawkcombe Head on Thursday. Love to Auntie & self from both*

Yes indeed I remember this spot. The postcard lists three magical places in the order in which they figured in my life – Malmsmead in the thirties, Oareford in the forties and Brendon Two Gates in the sixties and seventies.

My father longed for a wide open space, such as he had known in his childhood at Alston. He found it on Exmoor and most particularly at Malmsmead; already cashing in on Lorna Doone and supplementing the hard graft of sheep farming by shearing the growing chara-banc tourist trade. Here families from Bristol to the north and Exeter to the south, came by car to walk the moor and to learn to ride, but loads spilled from the charabancs to walk through a gate (3d) and head towards the Doone Valley. They weren't told how many miles that would involve and never made it. Much better spending time on a cream tea, buying postcards and a blue pottery jug with 'ow be yu' etched into the slip.

The sisters Mesdames Richards and Burge marketed themselves as Lorna Doone Farm and kept their husbands out of sight. Mrs Richards had the business acumen, was large and firmly fleshed to hug – being hugged by both sisters on arrival being part of the ritual – 'Oo mai dear, ow they've a'growed.' Mrs Burge was equally large but softer in character and in body, so much so that a direct frontal hug carried the risk of being engulfed in a bosom of clotted cream consistency.

Regular visitors, like us, ran out to find the men – well, to find Alf Burge first because he smelt of sheep and had dogs at foot and made fun of Mrs Richards. George Richards was lean and dour and tweedy, hiding any emotion behind a walrus moustache enriched by pipe smoke. Alf's smoking habit was home rolled fags which he stuck to his lip even when they were not alight.

Our contact with George Richards was daily, as he ran the stable of Hunters and Ponies. The board outside, in letters of sheep-dip-red clearly indicated that Hunters were 5/- an hour but that Ponies were only 2/6 an hour. Grand Parade, who was a Shetland Exmoor cross, could never be passed off as a hunter, nor could the broken down Colonel do service as a pony, but the reliable Daisy would serve as either. This rather depended on the size of the wallet that George had spied. Daisy was particularly reliable as she stopped, turned round and headed back to the stable when she reached the point that would get her back within the hour. Timid riders who had sworn at her for being a pony on the way up the valley, found that she returned to the stable as a hunter. Mum always chose Daisy but shrewd George never charged Dad other than pony price – for any of them.

I have been told that when a neighbouring farm, Southern Wood, came up for sale both George and Alf appeared at breakfast in their best market clothes but affected disinterest about the auction. They stood on opposite sides of the ring in Barnstaple Market later that morning. On the way home in the bus the man next to George turned to him and said, 'I hear Alf Burge bought Southern wood.' 'Aye, an George Richards made un paay for it.'

Mrs Richards had a Tuck Shop where she sold rationed sweets. I soon found that Crunchies, which were not allocated to the Exeter area, were available in the Bristol area, and that was certainly worth a hard hug.

Indoors Mrs Burge supervised the production of gargantuan meals. These were produced on an open wood fire by aged Tom whose white apron was changed at least once a month. Cooking took place in a backhouse attached to the old part of Malmsmead. In the corner away from the fire there built up a pile of chicken bones, discarded gristle, potato peelings and feathers from recent pluckings. It was a corner always full of scavenging activity and not only by the farm dogs. I used to take this route to the lean-to on the end of the newer part of Malmsmead where the Crunchies could be obtained.

We were waited on at table by either Annie who was gentle, ladylike and sweet with children, or Winnie who was none of these things. We soon knew her as Winnie-the Pooh and wrinkled our noses. Winnie had floated across from the Welsh Valleys and had a lilting voice – she clearly loved children and wished them to get closer to her. Unforgettable for me is Winnie's face when she observed a 'genelmun' casually putting a brown ten bob note on the silver collection plate at Oare church.

Soon after the war Mum and I got off a charabanc at County Gate and carried our cases down the steep path, crossing the East Lyn by a footbridge, to pay a final visit to Mesdames Richards and Burge.

Oareford
We rented the school house at Oareford for 5 shillings a week, for a few years before the War, when it was requisitioned for evacuees from Bristol, who hated it and ran back

home. Brian and I loved every moment spent there. We considered the whole of Chalk Water, joining Weir Water outside our door, a private river. Across the Chalk we threw an old barked larch for greasy pole balancing. This valley wasn't farmed before the war and ponies came down past the sheep dip, to graze between the gorse bushes up as far as Robber's Bridge. Above the bridge the road petered out to a stony track which even the shod ponies found difficult. Occasionally used for motor trials, it led out via Culbone Stables to the top of Porlock Hill. I learned to swim in a pool above the bridge and after fifty years revisited it with my mother. It was her last visit to Exmoor and deep thoughts came of happy days with George and her two boys. She sat in a folding chair beside the pool and neither of us spoke, though she was aware that we had come once more for me to say – thank you for this. As we packed up I mentioned walking from the cottage to Robber's Bridge at sunset and seeing a stag high above us on the skyline.

'George said it was a Royal Stag.'

'Of course it was, Mum.'

David is a retired Veterinary Surgeon (and a man of letters *Ed*), who believes that there may still be some who remember these places as fondly as he does and that the younger generation may find his recollections of historical interest. He adds, 'I have no wish to offend any descendants but I have been kinder towards the Burges, whose line continued from Alf through Jackie Burge, than to the Richards. Poor George, but I have a feeling that there may be no close relations that side.'

Badgworthy Water below Cloud Farm.

THE GREAT EXMOOR DEBATE –
A PERSONAL PERSPECTIVE

Hugh Thomas

In June 1976, the Exmoor National Park Officer, General Dare Wilson, left Exmoor House to fetch the Police to eject Guy Somerset, Chairman of the Exmoor Society, from the National Park Committee meeting. That incident was just one facet of a complete breakdown of relations between those involved in Exmoor.

The decade of the 1960s is remembered as the permissive years, but at the end they turned nasty; the "Summer of Love" gave way to student riots and the occupation of universities. The 1970s gave us the six-day war between Egypt and Israel, and the subsequent hike in oil prices, combined with militant miners unions, reduced the country to working only on three days in a week, the issuing of petrol ration books, 50 miles an hour speed limits on our roads and televisions shutting down at 10:30pm so that the nation would turn in early and save power. Edward Heath called an early election on the basis of "Who Governs Britain?" In South Africa there was the Sharpeville Massacre and, in Northern Ireland, "Bloody Sunday".

What was happening on Exmoor seemed to reflect the general context. Anger slowly built up and boiled over into threatening confrontation. In the background, national policies clashed between the Ministry of Agriculture's commitment to producing "Food from Our Own Resources" and the growing legislation for access to the countryside and conservation (which we then called "amenity"). While political power in Westminster swung from right to left and back again in frequent elections, rampant inflation and loss of the empire abroad led to a crisis of national self-confidence.

The Exmoor Society was born defending moorland. First, from a proposal to afforest The Chains (to prevent a repeat of the Lynmouth flood) and, secondly, to prevent agricultural improvement of rough grazings and moorland with a publication "Can Exmoor Survive?".

Most of Exmoor is eminently improvable for agricultural production. The Ministry of Agriculture (MAFF) valued the hills for their production of beef and lambs for finishing on lowland pastures in what was known as "the food chain". With the balance of payments deficit preoccupying politicians, the production of food at home to replace imports was a necessity as manufacturing industry failed to compete in exports. There were incentives directed at the improvement of British agriculture's efficiency by grant aid for capital improvements and support for prices through the annual agricultural price review being replaced by the European system of market intervention. Hill farms were given more support because of their inherent disadvantages of exposure, slope and poor soils. This meant that there were drainage grants, fencing grants, ploughing grants and increased headage payments when more stock could be carried on the land.

The farmers who are small independent businesses did not see themselves as in competition with each other but together responded to the signals given to them by government policy and the incentives that they were offered. The national interest and self-interest combined. If the housewives of the day were encouraged by soap powder manufacturers to compare the brilliance of their white washing on the line with that next door, the farmer's natural objective was to make two blades of grass grow where one grew before.

The Minister of Agriculture's definition of improvable land on Exmoor was probably too cautious. A much greater proportion could have been improved by modern farming methods since, for example, steep slopes were not such a problem with modern tractors and machinery, and it was also clear that ploughing was not the only method by which improvement could be brought about. Grazing pressure and the balance of the time of year when stocking might take place can have a progressive, minor, subtle and cumulative effect. New agrochemicals were coming onto the market. Paraquat (a chemical spray that kills all green growth) had been tested for ICI at Prayway Head (near Blackpits) in 1965 and other techniques were coming onto the market for the improvement of pastures.

In the same context, Access and Amenity were the objectives of other government departments with legislation in 1968 requiring notification to the authorities before conversion of rough grazing to agricultural land. The Countryside Act also made provision for "access agreements". In 1974, the Sandford report settled a question of priority between nature conservation and public access in favour of the claims of the environment. The Community Land Act of 1975 gave local authorities compulsory purchase powers, without a public inquiry, to purchase land and a hint of Land Nationalisation was in the air.

Matters that since "time immemorial" were considered to be entirely within the province of the farmer were becoming the subject of public debate, and decisions over their livelihoods were being taken by government departments directly opposed to the objectives of MAFF. These changes began cumulatively to impact upon the Exmoor farming community.

A section of moorland east of Countisbury had been fenced and reseeded to grassland in 1962 but an attempt to have the area along the road between Lynmouth and County Gate made subject to planning control (which would have prevented fencing) was refused by the Minister for Housing and Local Government as "he was not satisfied that the circumstances justify the control sought".

Somerset County Council attempts to have powers to control ploughing inserted in the 1968 Countryside Act (the "Somerset proposals" which would have given the National Park Authority "amenity conservation orders") did not succeed in making its way through the Parliamentary process. SCC's application for a compulsory purchase order to secure public access at Lype Hill was declined in 1973 because of insufficient evidence of need. It was "important for the public's enjoyment of the National Park that there should continue to be reasonably friendly relations between Exmoor and Brendon Hill farmers and the rest of the community and… introduction of compulsory acquisition in a case where the need is not patent might jeopardise this relationship throughout the Park".

However, Exe Cleave (between Simonsbath and Exford) was partly improved from moorland after notification had been given to the Somerset Committee in 1972 before unification. For 2½ years, negotiations hammered out a proposal that would compensate the farmer and preserve the moorland vegetation but when it was put to the new Committee they rejected it. The farmer naturally felt that he had been unfairly treated by being prevented from his agricultural improvement over that period of time and for all the abortive costs of his own and professional representation in negotiating the terms that were recommended. This experience did nothing but harm to relations between the farmers and the conservationists. The National Park Committee (unified from the two County Councils in 1974) became the battleground.

It was becoming necessary to articulate the mechanics of the farming system in the hills and uplands. This was very poorly understood by those seeking to intervene. The problem is that these systems are not easily codified. Traditional methods had been handed down from generation to generation and local knowledge was acquired by narrative derived from experiments and initiatives, where they had failed or succeeded. Constant adaptation to changing climate and weather conditions are natural to people whose every day is spent exposed to the elements and not so well understood by people in offices.

Where the National Park attempted to gather this insight, their laudable attempts failed because the people who went on to the farms were asking the wrong questions and misunderstanding the answers. One such misunderstanding appeared in National Park papers as "high phosphate application" when what the farmer had said was "glyphosate application". It may be assumed that the farmer said glyphosate instead of Roundup to the Ph.D. qualified botanist because he was attempting to adapt to the sort of terms used by his interrogator. There was a general failure to communicate.

In a letter to *The Times*, I drew attention to the counterintuitive but disastrous contrast between the labour costs of extensive hill farming compared with the same rates of pay applied to lowland farming enterprises. The output generated by £100 of labour cost is miniscule by comparison with the output of labour from intensive farming on the lowlands. Thus it is that farm workers are much more expensive to use in a hill farming situation and farmers themselves have a much lower standard of living. We argued that hill and upland farmers should be treated no worse than lowland farmers ("barley barons" as they were then called) just because they strive to make their living in the most difficult of soils, climate and topography.

1976 saw a series of events that became known as The Battle for Exmoor from a *Sunday Telegraph* headline. The first of these was the Phillips Report. The National Park Officer approached a Scottish practitioner of moorland management to report on the state of

Exmoor's heather and grass moors. John Phillips wrote his controversial views as a private report for General Wilson. Its approach to the southern grass moors (molinia grass) was heavily influenced by the Scottish context for the management of grouse. Its publication was demanded by Malcolm MacEwen (Secretary of State appointee to the National Park Committee, and Exmoor Society Committee member) on the basis that it had been paid for out of public money but it was delayed until a revised draft was circulated together with my own submission dealing with the management of the molinia grazing areas.

In August 1976, the Exmoor National Park Consultative Draft Plan was published but it too was controversial. It was caught up in the controversy over the purchase of Stowey Allotment. Malcolm MacEwen complained to Peter Shore (Secretary of State for the Environment) about a "kangaroo court" in which he had been held to account for leaking details of the National Park's confidential discussions. The Consultative Draft was withdrawn before the end of the year.

Stowey Allotment was a small but significant area of moorland, visible from Brendon Common and on the A39 coast road from Porlock to Lynton, and was offered for sale in 1976. The National Park Committee decided to buy it if they could, to preserve its landscape appearance, or for Public Access if this would be the only acceptable purpose for the public money to be allocated. The procedures for a public body to expend funds require that the County Valuer should advise the maximum price that represents fair value. The amount the County Valuer thought he could justify and would be sufficient to achieve a purchase was informed by past sales and discussions with the owner, but while the price may have reflected the current use value it did not take into account the potential that could be realised by conversion of the land to a more intensive type of grassland with the aid of grants and subsidies available to all farmers in the UK – without differentiation for National Park designation.

Farmer members of the ENP Committee were well aware of the potential value of Stowey Allotment but the County Valuer's opinion in these questions is what binds the freedom of action of an acquiring authority. Despite their insight, the amount authorised was insufficient and at the auction no bid on behalf of Exmoor National Park could be entered as part of the auction process as it progressed to a successful bid of £35,000 for the 375 acres. This proved to be a costly missed opportunity for the Park. By April 1977, a management plan for Stowey Allotment had been discounted following prior notice of intention to improve the grazing and the way to plough the land had been cleared.

As a former Political Correspondent for the *Daily Worker*, Malcolm MacEwen had the necessary skills and contacts to goad his opponents, the local representatives on the National Park Committee, and draw attention nationally to what *The Times* referred to as the "Growing Heat" on Exmoor. The Park Committee was in permanent state of tension. Minutes were routinely challenged so audio equipment was installed for the benefit of note takers.

On 28th September 1976, Ben Halliday (Vice Chairman of the Committee) wrote to General Wilson (the National Park Officer) with an analysis of the principal conflicts of interest between agriculture and amenity and nature conservation involving reclamation, public path relocation and proposing five diversion orders at Glenthorne. The Exmoor Society objected to four diversion orders. Early in 1977, Ben Halliday proposed a "multiple land use" management plan. This eminently sensible suggestion which involved concessions on all sides with the objective of satisfying, so far as possible, the requirements of nature conservation, public access and sustainable economics was a new approach and eventually became the key to the resolution of the conflict. At the time it was hotly contested.

A fruitful source of dispute was the collection of statistics for the area of moorland at any given date and the supposed loss at so much per year which, if extrapolated, would lead to the total erosion of Exmoor's moor and heath. These statistics are bandied about still but the success of the eventual resolution of the conflict renders them of minor importance now. Suffice it to say that the exaggeration of any of the issues in contention at this time was used to exacerbate the Great Exmoor Debate and Thesis v Antithesis were collided to provoke a Synthesis in classic mode.

Into this state of near uproar, the Government interposed with an Inquiry led by Lord Porchester who had very good experience of the workings of County Councils in a personal capacity. A great deal of evidence was submitted by all the interested parties.

Lord Porchester's Report when it was published established that there were 40,000 acres of critical amenity moorland of which at that time, 12,000 acres were owned by local Authorities or the National Trust, plus 8,000 acres that were owned as subject to common rights. Of the remaining 20,000 acres two estates controlling large areas had no intention to improve moorland.

Porchester's Report was tailored for Exmoor but it set out the ground rules that were subsequently incorporated into legislation. Principally, these included the collection of information about the location and extent of moorland vegetation types, and a second map of those where the policies of the Park Authority are to be directed to preserve for all time the character of the landscape.

The problem remained, however, about the farmers' freedom of action to win a living from their own land and the national interest of producing food to replace imports, and the national interest in preserving the character of the National Park, as advanced locally by the Exmoor Society. Lord Porchester's solution was for a long stop compulsory Moorland Conservation Order. This had all the defects of negativism but it very nearly became law. The story of how the voluntary system progressed from there will follow in the 2015 Review, but it did save Exmoor from the plough.

Exmoor Land Agent for 45 years, Hugh Thomas has been involved with the business of farming moorland and managing estates for the largest private landowners on Exmoor, involved with extensive areas of great conservation interest.

EXMOOR BIRDS – LOSSES AND GAINS

David Ballance

If some boffin were to provide me with a reliable time machine, my first order to it would be to drop me on Black Barrow, at dawn on a fine early summer's day in 1800. I would walk from there across the Forest to Wood Barrow, turn south to Moles Chamber and then east along the ridgeway to Dulverton. I could then discover something of the birds of the Moor before the Knights began their work in the 1820s. I might meet a mounted shepherd up from Oare, or even Colonel Bassett's newly-entered hounds (who hunted hinds all through May that year after the ravages of distemper), and I could interrogate the last inhabitant of Badgworthy Village, Mr Tucker, who is to perish in a snowstorm fifteen years later.

As it is, we know almost nothing about Exmoor birds before the 1880s. A few great rarities were seen and later appeared in glass cases: a White-tailed Eagle about 1870 (still to be seen in Lynton Museum); a curious, and possibly American, melanistic Rough-legged Buzzard, and an American Bittern, both in 1875; a Snowy Owl in 1876. From about 1865, James Turner, a hunting man from a Staplegrove family, made notes, which were published in 1912, and which included two Golden Plover nests on the Forest. He noted the surprising number of Marsh Harrier specimens; they may have bred in those pre-drainage days (as they did in Ireland). We know that about four Hen Harrier clutches were taken before 1914, and the first Merlin's nest was found in Hoccombe Water in 1907.

The gates of tourism had been opened by the popularity of *Lorna Doone* in 1869 and by the coming of the railways to Minehead in 1874 and to Lynton in 1898. The first car climbed Porlock Hill in 1900, but until the 1920s few naturalists penetrated the Moor, and hardly anyone went beyond the Whitstones-Exford road. Yet the tragic young Barnstaple naturalist Bruce Cummings (later struck down by multiple sclerosis and author of *Journal of a Disappointed Man*) was able to explore the western tip of the Moor and the valleys round Lynton, where he found the surviving Buzzards targeted by egging workmen. One notable visitor, Edmund Selous, the inventor of the word "bird-watching", stayed at Bossington in 1909, and made a carefully prepared visit to Black Grouse leks: he left his lodgings at two a.m. and rode or pushed his bike up to Hillhead Cross to watch the birds coming through the rain over a beech hedge.

Ernest Hendy, whose works became nationally famous after the First World War, largely confined his explorations to the Dunkery area. His Exmoor still had regular Merlins, two species of Grouse (Red were introduced in 1916 and soon prospered), Curlew and Ring Ouzels. We know little of Exmoor birds in the Second World War, when large areas were inaccessible, though Dunkery remained open, and even in the bird-watching boom which followed the lifting of petrol rationing, most observers were to be found in the eastern combes, where Chetsford Water could yield all the best species in an hour or two. John Coleman Cooke, the founder of the Exmoor Society, actually lived at Simonsbath for two periods between 1952 and 1966, and was able to add to our very thin knowledge of birds on the Forest.

By the 1970s, both species of Grouse were in decline. Red Grouse were no longer keepered and Blackcock, as everywhere in southern England, could no longer cope with multiple threats: disturbance, fencing, the loss of key areas along the boundary between the moor and the farmland (such as the reclamations along the west side of Nutscale), and Pheasant-rearing in the Culbone Hill plantations. I saw what I believe was the last Grey Hen in Chetsford, silhouetted against the evening glow on the night of the Prince of Wales's wedding, 29 July 1981. The National Park unsuccessfully attempted introductions, and the last birds from these were seen in Devon about 1987. In the 1990s, Red Grouse speedily declined; the last were probably on Brendon Common, where they had originally been released, about 2007.

Such disappearances and concerns about the dwindling numbers of Merlins, Curlews and Ring Ouzels made it desirable to acquire a better knowledge of bird populations on the whole Moor. In summer 1978 a pioneer survey of target species was carried out by S. Davies and R. Jarman for the RSPB and what was then the Somerset Trust for Nature Conservation. This has been followed by three further surveys, in 1992/93, 2002 and 2008, all under RSPB control. Improvements have been steadily made in the methods used, and it has become possible to monitor trends. These surveys have covered all the open moorland, where reclamation and additional drainage have now virtually ceased. Woodland and farmland have not been entirely neglected, and some areas of these have been looked at in other years, such as the Porlock Vale and the new NNRs in the Barle Valley woodlands. Space does not here allow a full account of their findings, but some of the most important points can be given.

A few species which have declined widely over southern England have continued to flourish on the Moor. Cuckoos show no decline here, perhaps because of the abundance of the Meadow Pipit "hosts" and of large caterpillars. The numbers of Whinchats astonished local observers in 1978, but the majority are in grass moorland west of the Exford road, which Minehead-based watchers have often neglected; there were 411 territories in 2008. Reed Buntings seem to have colonised Exmoor (and Dartmoor) in an unobtrusive way about fifty years ago; there were 206 territories in 2008. Willow Warblers, conspicuous by song along moorland edges, remain very common, with 958 territories, though they have almost vanished from much of lowland Somerset.

Others have not done so well. Wheatears have declined; they are faithful to a few sites, such as Upper Hoaroak Water, but are hard to find elsewhere, though they have never been very numerous, as they are on Dartmoor. Ring Ouzels have evidently ceased to breed, the last proof having been in 2002, though they still occur on both passages; and Curlew, for some years reduced to a few pairs on the heather moorland of the north-east and on North Molton Common, seem now to have vanished. In the last six years, only one Merlin site has been certainly occupied. The figures for some other "Exmoor" species which largely belong to non-moorland habitats are more difficult to interpret:

Dippers have probably declined, perhaps because of stock barriers across rivers; Grey Wagtails have recently suffered a setback from hard winters, despite their being mainly summer visitors at higher levels; and Redstarts seem to have dwindled in moorland combes, but not necessarily in woodland or around upland farms.

The last twenty years have seen the arrival of two new species. Goosanders colonised the Barle in 1993, and have spread to the Exe. Dartford Warblers appeared in the Western Gorse on Robin How in 1995 and spread rapidly to many sites; by 2008 there were thought to be about 150 territories. Unfortunately, as non-migrants, they are vulnerable to heavy snow cover, and were almost wiped out by two hard winters. There have been slight signs of recovery near the coast, but there are now only a handful of pairs.

Woodland birds are more difficult to assess. Many good sites are either private or inaccessible or both. Pied Flycatchers have been lured by nest-boxes to a number of places; there are major schemes in Horner Woods, in Hawk Combe and elsewhere, of which the most intensive is in Barlynch Woods, where in 2012 74 birds were fledged from 23 breeding attempts. Two species have greatly declined: Marsh Tits are now scarce, and as they are very sedentary, gaps in the population are not easily filled; and Lesser Spotted Woodpeckers are dangerously close to extinction, except in Horner. The numbers of Wood Warblers, which up to twenty years ago were abundant in sessile oakwoods with a sparse shrub layer, have shrunk alarmingly, perhaps through problems in their African winter quarters or on migration.

There have been two recent developments in recording. The first is the launching of the Exmoor Bird Monitoring Project, an informal partnership between amateurs and professionals, whose members walk fourteen routes annually between 15 May and 15 June, and report on a range of target species. This has ensured that regular observation is maintained during the years between the big RSPB surveys in areas which otherwise might be neglected, especially along the Exe and Barle, round the headwaters of Badgworthy, on Devon Exmoor and on Worth Hill. Thus we have been made aware of the fall in Stonechat numbers and of the stability of the Cuckoo population. The scheme has now run for seven years. The second development is connected with the Mires Project, run by David Smith for South West Water, which has recreated boggy areas on the plateau by building small dams and blocking drains, with a view to retaining potential flood waters on the higher ground. In some places this has resulted in small ponds, as can now be seen at Exe Head and on the west side of the Blackpitts-Brendon Two Gates road. A survey carried out by David Boyce in 2011/12 has shown that these have helped to maintain the small numbers of breeding Snipe and it has provided further evidence of the presence of many Grasshopper Warblers. These are steadily buzzing away at dawn and dusk in long heather and tussock grassland, but they fall silent during the daytime. The 2008 Survey found an amazing 300 territories.

In the conifers, Siskins are now regular breeders in many places, as can be seen in late summer when parents bring their young to feeders. Crossbills are late-winter breeders, and the mature plantations on the Brendons have allowed the establishment of a permanent population.

Lastly, mention must be made of some rarer species. Red Kites, which were persecuted to extinction by 1850, have been seen in some numbers during the last few years, mainly in late spring. Many of these are young pioneers from the hugely expanded native Welsh population, or from introductions in the Midlands, but at least some have probably drifted over from France. Two breeding attempts have been made so far in Somerset, of which one was near Dulverton. Neither was successful, but it cannot be long before they settle with us. There have also been summer sightings of Hen Harriers, and Hobbies have been seen frequently around the edges of the Moor. In most recent winters one or two Great Grey Shrikes have spent several months in the Dunkery and Chetsford combes.

Much of the Moor, away from north-east and the main roads, is very little trodden. Between 2000 and 2007, I made 150 visits, spread over every week of the year, on a circuit walk up Weir Water, over Black Barrow and down Chalk Water, and I recorded every bird seen: among them, 4,528 Carrion Crows, four Dotterel and one Greenfinch. Each walk lasted about three hours. I met only 26 people and two dogs; from 1 October to 31 March I saw nobody at all, and if I had met the Beast, only the Ravens might have found the remains.

Readers of this article can be very helpful in reporting their sightings. The following contacts are useful:

The Bird Recorder for the Exmoor Natural History Society is Roger Butcher: Ashdown, East Anstey, Tiverton EX16 9JJ; 01398 341 766. This Society covers the area of the National Park in both counties and publishes records annually in *The Exmoor Naturalist*.

The Recorder for the Somerset Ornithological Society is Brian Gibbs: 23 Lyngford Road, Taunton TA2 7EE; 01823 274887/ brian.gibbs@virgin.net. There is also a website for the Society: www.somersetbirds.net. Records are published annually in *Somerset Birds* (of which recent copies can be obtained from me at £9.00 incl. p. & p.).

Devon records can be handled by ENHS, but they can also be sent to Julia Harris: 6 Clonway, Yelverton PL20 6EG; 01822 853785/ devon-recorder@lycos.com. Records are published annually in *The Devon Bird Report*.

Or you can always contact me: Flat Two, Dunboyne, Bratton Lane, Minehead TA24 8SQ/ 01643 706820.

Copies of *The Birds of Exmoor and the Quantocks*, by Brian Gibbs and me, can usually be obtained from Rothwell and Dunworth's bookshop at Dulverton. It was published in 2003, and is now showing its age!

David Ballance lives in Minehead. Although he spent his working life as a schoolmaster in Essex, he has had an Exmoor base for 67 years. The author of *A History of the Birds of Somerset*, he edited The Annual Somerset Bird Report for many years and is presently working with others on the Atlas of Somerset Birds.

A HIDDEN GEM IN AN EXMOOR PARISH CHURCH – THE RESTORATION OF AN HISTORIC ORGAN AT BROMPTON REGIS

William Rees

In 1897 the parishioners of the Exmoor village of Brompton Regis, near Dulverton, marked the Diamond Jubilee of Queen Victoria with a heroic fund-raising effort to buy a church organ of great quality. Though the population in those days was larger than it is now the village was far from wealthy, and parish ledgers of the period show a significant number of people in receipt of charitable support from church endowments. The project was led by the recently appointed Rev. William Batchelor, an evidently dynamic and persuasive character, and was bolstered by sponsorship including a substantial donation from "an anonymous lady friend of the Vicar". Church and press records of the time reveal no more about her identity, but recent research suggests that she is likely to have been a member of the Courage brewing family.

The organ builder was the distinguished T.C. Lewis, a technologically innovative leader of the craft whose creations included the Southwark Cathedral organ. He was based in south London, close to William Batchelor's previous parish at Horsleydown in Southwark and to the nearby Courage headquarters. It is known that the brewery firm sponsored both the company and a number of its clients, and one member of the family, John Michell Courage, served as Lewis's financial controller in the 1890s. By a remarkable coincidence a branch of the Courages was to settle in 1947 at Redcross Farm, Brompton Regis, though a surviving member of that generation (now living in Taunton and an inheritor of the family's love of organ music) is unable to confirm a family involvement with the village 50 years earlier.

Lewis first built our classic organ in 1872, for "a gentleman" who also remains anonymous, though research into his identity has not been abandoned. This suggests that it was supplied for a large house rather than a church. The gentleman returned it to Lewis in 1896 in part exchange for a bigger instrument (so perhaps it was a particularly large house), and after refurbishment the instrument came to Brompton Regis at a total cost of £350. As the date of the installation service arrived the parish was £7 short of the total, but that shortfall was made up by the collection on the day.

The installation on Easter Monday 1897 was a great occasion, reported in elaborate detail in the *West Somerset Free Press* on April 24th. The account opens with a reference to "an organ of which many much larger churches would be proud", and lists all the music played and sung during the service. There were distinguished ecclesiastical figures and other guests (including unnamed visitors from London) among a packed congregation. An inspiring sermon on the importance of music in worship was preached by Dr Edmund Warre, the Head Master of Eton College, and much of it is recorded in the article. He spent his holidays at the Baronsdown estate near Brompton Regis (the once-grand house built close to the ruins of Barlynch Priory no longer exists, sadly), and he endowed the fine altar window in the church. After the service there were peals of bells and a splendid tea for all the parishioners.

Despite a partial overhaul and clean in 1962 the organ has deteriorated considerably through a further half century, and its complex inner workings are now dust-clogged

and desiccated, wheezing and rusting. Though it is semi-playable at present with periodic maintenance, it has become clear that its future working life would be very limited without major renovation. Scrapping it is unthinkable, and the PCC decided in 2012 (the corresponding year of our own Queen's reign, very appropriately) to embark on a full and authentic restoration project, in order to preserve organ music in the church for present and future generations, and to honour and emulate the achievement of our predecessors back in 1897.

Experts who have examined it have been thrilled to find in a small Exmoor parish a structurally unspoilt example of the work of T.C. Lewis (many church organs have been modified and modernised, not always appropriately), and have described it as "a hidden gem" and "a Rolls-Royce of an instrument". The leading contemporary expert on Lewis organs was among them; he did not previously know of its existence, but confirmed its authenticity. It has recently been awarded a Historic Organ Certificate by the British Institute of Organ Studies. When restored as nearly as possible to its original condition, our two-manual instrument will have recovered the power and tonal quality for which Lewis was renowned.

Nicholas Pevsner's book on English churches records in 1947 "a pretty organ case in the arts and crafts style, with golden floral motifs on a black background". Sadly that was removed or painted over at some point between then and the 1962 overhaul. There are still a few in the community who remember it, but not the precise reason for its disappearance. They include two who in their youth used to pump the organ for services before electricity arrived in 1962, and they tell with some glee the story of a third who caused a scandal when he fell asleep during a long sermon, with a deafening silence as the result when the next hymn was announced. By the 1950s the church had unfortunately become very run-down and damp, and the strongest theory is that the decorated wooden case had deteriorated along with the general fabric of the building, which was then rescued through major work by the Rev. W.D. Speakman in the 1960s (a good deal of it with his own hands).

The dismantling and restoration work will take place through the 2013-14 autumn and winter. Fundraising towards the expected cost of £28,000 has been under way since September 2012, and by June 2013 £21,000 had already been raised. Further support in the form of grants and donations from charitable trusts, organisations and interested individuals will be welcomed by a small Exmoor parish for which this project is a considerable challenge. For a further update on the fund with information on the organ and its restoration please see www.bromptonregis.com/organ

After a career as a House Master and then Tutor for Admissions at Eton College, together with editing and translation work including the Penguin Book of French Poetry, William Rees has retired to Brompton Regis, where to his surprise he has learned by trial and much error to play the organ. He has loved Exmoor since boyhood holidays, which included tagging along on Jones family visits to Hope Bourne (see the 2012 Review).

HOPE BOURNE COMPETITION 2012/2013

Judges' Comments

Again this year the judges found much to enjoy in the forty or so entries – whether focusing on landscape, weather, human behaviour or the observation of a single bird or animal. That famous command of Ezra Pound – 'Make it new' – is a constant challenge, especially in writing about the natural world. Can there be anything new to say, even to see? But of course there is, because there is always a new pair of eyes seeing it, and a new consciousness responding to the rhythms of the year and to the pulse of the written/spoken line.

All good poems delight us by how, as well as what, they show us, whether Hardy's thrush 'in blast-beruffled plume' or Alice Oswald's 'Stone Skimmer' who 'brushes / the restless thistles, their dried skins hooked to their bones'. In these submissions we were glad to find poems that could hold together such detail and delight within a structure, sturdy but not inflexible – whether with or without rhyme and stanza-form – and poems that didn't peter out but reached a confident end. Some poems started strongly but became repetitive or banal; some delivered a 'message' too baldly, not leaving the reader space to infer it. One or two poems were not about Exmoor at all: do read the rules when you enter a competition!

There were individual details of observation that struck us: 'rain bursts on the hills like shot' ('Toll Road (I)') and 'the path we took / was split by a spine of grass' ('On Exmoor'). Other unexpected comparisons that provided a little shock of pleasure were 'wits sharpened like the air whetting its blunt edge' ('X'), and trees seen through mist 'with the switched-on clarity of an X-ray screen' ('January Trees'). We'd also like to commend 'The Edge of Exmoor'.

Our final choices are, in third place, 'A Line through Exmoor', an ambitious poem full of vigorous striking images which make the reader see the 'Line' across the landscape. The form – an unrhymed sestina – enacts in its language and rhythms the labour of the walk, though we felt there was a bit of over-working on occasion (and we queried the word 'wend' in the fifth stanza). Second place went to 'Snatches of the Moor' – another ambitious choice of form with its alternating tercets and couplets, some vivid sharp observation of shape, colour and movement, haunting use of assonance and a beautiful closing phrase. Just occasionally the writing slips towards the rhetorical, as if the poet doesn't quite trust the observation. The winning poem, 'Doe at Horner Woods' impressed us by its unusual point of view, the daring plunge into an animal's consciousness and scent-world, the inventiveness of language, the shift of scale from the doe to the universe of stars and planets, and the sudden awareness of the watching human presence at the end. There was a confident use of couplets and, among a variety of musical effects, the strong swoops of some enjambed lines.

Congratulations to the winners, and many thanks to the entrants for giving us so much pleasure in reading your work.

Liz Berry and Christine Webb

One of the judges was the first person last year to identify Helen Mort's poem 'The Deer' as having been submitted by another writer, with only minor alterations. We have been particularly careful to check this year's entries, and have put the titles and key lines from the winning poems into a search engine. Nothing has been identified as previously published.

Editor

Photograph of Hope Lilian Bourne at Lanacre Bridge.

DOE AT HORNER WOODS

Cristina Navazo-Eguia Newton

The clearest path is the one I follow by the tug of musk
daubed on the bark of oaks, the heather and the moss.

The breeze turns and I can see by the hidden codes of scents.
Even in the dark they sing their pristine notes: who was it,

what they were up to, how long ago. If we had names
like humans do, I'd be able to tell 'Red Stag the Wise Strut'

grazed this grass three hours ago; 'Sister Doe Flit' drank
from this puddle close to dawn and she was warm. She left

a downy-silver-scuttle-lichen-dewdrop-three-word-sentence
of a smell, her unique tag. And in the wake of it,

a brimming-moon-sway-sop-twelve-week-fawn-glow.
Her thin-air toe-gait carried the sighs of rained-on earth.

My mind tunes to the slightest twitch. I read the eyelash
flick of every blade of grass, the neat calligraphy of twigs

talking sense behind my back, which blurs if they are still
into a dunce flat mat. But what stops for long? The stars

pour to the west; the planet's magnetic streams swish
underground; spring slides through the growing trees and

sap pumps from their roots to their bursting buds.
The anxious leaves suck air, then spit it out. I hear it all:

your breath, your heart in your mouth, the lifting of your hand.

SNATCHES OF THE MOOR
Sarah James

In stubbled grass, stags arch.
Sparked clouds held high, patches
of sky hang from their antlers.

> here now, here then, a hand meets
> a hand, and curves to frame it

A brush of dark trees. Blue daubs
at blanched winter borders.
Snow rubs the moor's feet.

> the tracks of once footprints
> follow, dissect, intermingle

Anchored, ships in the harbour await
tide-time's holler. Beguiled, they slip
loose, sift to and from shore greenness.

> this sound fluted into our bones
> knows the edge of heathered silence

Into the mist that is sunlight and slopes.
The landscape elopes, then re-emerges,
shape firmed by its shadows.

> stand back from your tautest cliff,
> lift from the rivers, pause in time with the curlew

A LINE THROUGH EXMOOR

Cristina Navazo-Eguia Newton
On Richard Long's abstract 'walking sculpture'

This work of his, like the wind, is invisible,
so he draws the theory in pencil – a straight line
on a compass bearing of 290 degrees –
with a ruler across the Ordnance Survey map.
It'll be a sculpture of strides on the terrain,
north-west to south-east, from Parracombe to Exford.

It means a radical departure from his previous *Line
Made by Walking*, a piece of grounded pith:
see the bare thread worn in the meadow
by his tread from A to B, backwards
and forwards for a month, in this photograph
taken before the grass grew back.

 But *A Line through Exmoor* will leave no trace
other than his memories of it, wearing thin
and thinner with each day, and what appears
on paper as a neat, hassle-free bee-shot,
like a biography of the artist in a hundred words,
translates as miles of fences, hedges, banks.

All the trundling through moors under the rain,
scrambles over styles, the slosh through fords,
the sludge in bogs, the clods loading his soles,
traipsing ice-hardened soil, thirst, breath clouding
in the frost, the steep combes, the trespassing,
wire fences, foxes' holes, the arrow-like

line in his mind will need to rhyme in slant.
His progress will wend the corrugated verse
of a space odyssey told in rambling phrases
his heart understands but cannot speak.
He'll pause under the sleek antiphonies of owls,
in the ruffled waves of red stags' bellows,

the ultrasound fizz of damselflies, the drone
of easterlies harassing the uplands' face,
breaking through the boundary of his scheme.

Leigh Falls.
PHOTO BY JUDY MOSS

CHALLENGES IN MANAGING EXMOOR WOODLANDS

Ben Williams

The Badgworthy Land Company is an organisation set up between the two world wars to preserve and enhance Exmoor's sporting heritage. The Company is still dedicated to the encouragement of participation in outdoor sporting pursuits. Over the years the Company has been gifted areas of land to further these aims. The majority is made up of large areas of open moorland, but includes farm land and a substantial body of woodland. The ownership of land brings the responsibility of managing the land and in this article I will describe how the Badgworthy Land Company manages its woodland.

The Company owns woodland in large blocks of several hundred acres through to small bits of infill between fields of less than half an acre. The type of woodland ranges from commercial conifer crops through to ancient woodland of oak, ash and hazel and other native broadleaf species, while some are grazed woodlands unfenced from the moorland or grassland adjacent to them. All of the woodland falls within the Exmoor National Park (ENP) and some of it is designated as areas of Special Scientific Interest (SSSI). Some is hidden away and is unlikely to be seen by most people whereas some is very visible having major walking routes including the Two Moors Way and the Coleridge Way running through them. The Company owns much of Snowdrop Valley which some of you may have visited when the road is closed to traffic in February because of the numbers attracted to the spectacle.

The Company aims to protect its woodland but does not try to make a living out of the income. This gives the Company considerable latitude to do, either, nothing for long periods of time, or, only conservation enhancing activities. Because of the sensitive nature of some of the sites the Company works very closely with the ENP forestry officers and Natural England to devise management plans that bring out the potential of the woodland.

A recent example of this is a programme of invasive beech control in woodland in the Barle Valley both above and below Tarr Steps. This was a three year programme to prevent beech becoming over-dominant in what was largely an oak coppice landscape created by the tan bark industry and later taken over by the pit prop industry. Whilst doing this work extra effort was put in to raise the light levels for some of the rare West Country lichens which survive in the ultra pollution free environment that we are lucky enough to enjoy. Some of these lichens need the extra light that traditional coppice management used to provide. The extra light that reaches the woodland floor also increases the wildflower numbers and variety to be found. Although a small amount of timber was extracted for commercial reasons, most of the trunks and limbs were left in place, having been cross cut to make them safe, to break down naturally and provide a food source for insects which in turn will become part of the food chain.

Cutcombe Wood

Another example of active management that is in the middle of a three year programme is an effort to eradicate rhododendron ponticum in the woodlands at Cutcombe (next to Snowdrop Valley). We have completed the first year in this effort. Although the rhododendron may flower beautifully in May/June it is a thuggish plant that crowds out the understory, preventing other plants from growing, including the regeneration of tree saplings that die from lack of light. There is also evidence that Rhododendron produces a chemical that inhibits the ability of other plants to grow which allows it to take over given enough time. This effect remains in the ground even after the rhododendron has been killed and it can be some years before a healthy understory returns. Getting rid of rhododendron is no easy matter as it seems to rise from the dead like the worst sort of zombie film. At Cutcombe we have used three different methods, including hand chopping and stump painting, spraying for smaller growth and finally injecting herbicide directly into the stem base. The first and last method are very labour intensive but have a better record of effectiveness than spraying alone.

Another piece of woodland management that the Company has been obliged to do last winter is a clearfell of two blocks of Japanese Larch. These had fallen victim to the disease *Phytophthora Ramorum* known colloquially as Sudden Oak Death. This is an example of alien diseases that can cut a swath through our woodlands and they have different effects in different climates. This one, paradoxically, does no harm to our oaks but has proven disastrous to Larch which was thought immune until the first instance in 2009. Since then it has found the south west, with its warm wet climate, the ideal breeding ground.

Stacked infected Larch.

Following the receipt of an European disease order the company was obliged to fell the entire stand of about 10 acres about 10-15 years before the crop reached maturity. It is quite a waste when one thinks of the effort in planting and waiting for this to happen. As it turned out the Company was able to find a purchaser who had a licence to process the timber for woodchip. The winter after next someone will be kept warm.

The Company does not have any employees so all the work that is undertaken is done by outside contractors. The skills of woodland management are as much a part of our heritage as the landscape and the built environment. With this in mind the Company attempts to use local contractors for all its work and for all the operations described above only local Exmoor people have been used. This preserves the skills and provides employment that can help to keep people on Exmoor.

Woodland management is a long term process and does not work if a quick profit is required. The Badgworthy Land Company has been looking after some very important Exmoor woodland for the last 90 years and aims to continue for at least another 90.

Ben Williams returned to Exmoor after working for most of his life in the city. After retraining at the Royal Agricultural College in 2007, he has worked in The Elms Estate Office, Bishop's Tawton where he is involved in looking after a number of rural clients including The Badgworthy Land Company.

MARY CHUGG – ARTIST AND FOUNDER MEMBER

Jenny Gibson

One of my major regrets about being a relatively newcomer to Exmoor is that many of the noteworthy Exmoor characters were no longer with us by the time I arrived, meaning that I have got to know about them only through what I have read or what other people have told me. Brian Chugg, an early member of the Exmoor Society and a locally renowned artist, author and lecturer, is one of those people. I have thoroughly enjoyed going through a collection of his photographic slides, which his widow Mary has kindly given to the Society, and linking some of them with excerpts from his field notebooks written during the winter of 1963. The ensuing article is reproduced in this Review on page 17.

Mary Chugg, however, is very much alive and my husband Tony and I were delighted to be able to spend an afternoon with her at her home in Bishops Tawton. Quite by chance, it was the 10th anniversary of Brian's death and this, instead of tingeing our interview with

View from Mary Chugg's sitting room at Bishop's Tawton – oil.

sadness, seemed to add a special piquancy to the occasion. Mary knows to the exact day how long it is since their wedding day and we could not help but feel moved by such a long, close and on-going relationship. Brian is everywhere around you in the house, for his paintings hang in virtually every room. Indeed, the house almost resembles an art gallery, filled with pictures and works of art not just by herself and Brian but by friends and fellow artists whose work the couple have admired and collected over the decades.

'Exmoor, Dartmoor – and the coast – were the background to our marriage,' Mary says, as she pours us tea and offers us slices of the most delicious, home-made cake that – incredibly – turns out to contain beetroot, something neither of us normally eat but, on this occasion, happily accept a second helping.

She is an attractive lady, who looks younger than she is. But this is not just her appearance, it is her personality. All the time we were with her, I am aware that she is someone who is always looking out at the world around her, not in at herself.

Brian came from an old Devonian family, whose history has been traced back 600 years. Mary is almost a Devonian. Her family moved from Bristol to Barnstaple, when she was just 18 months old. After attending Barnstaple Girls Grammar School, Mary went to Bath Academy of Art in Corsham. 'It was a wonderful place to be at that time when there were so many new things happening in the art world. We were very fortunate in having many of the well known painters of that time as our tutors, including those from St Ives, Cornwall.' Both her parents were interested in the arts and when her father retired from commercial travelling they opened a small antiques shop in Woolacombe. Much later on, her parents and the business moved to Braunton. In 1972, after teaching art at the Marist Convent in Barnstaple for eighteen years, Mary inherited the business and ran it, with great enjoyment, for twenty-three years.

She met Brian while she was a student and they married immediately after she left art school in 1955. Nine years her elder, Brian had spent a couple of years in an architectural practice, then become an art teacher, lecturing at North Devon College from 1953 to 1979. Mary says that she learnt a lot from him and their travels together, particularly about the history of art and painting techniques, which had not taken priority on her course at Corsham.

The couple lived in Barnstaple until 1981 then moved to Sharlands House in Braunton, built especially for Dr Elliston Wright – the doctor who actually delivered Brian – until 1997, when they moved to Bishops Tawton. Not long after this Brian developed rheumatoid arthritis, which increasingly took its toll on his activities.

Mary was a founder member of the Exmoor Society. She explains how in the spring of 1958, they became aware of a proposal to plant conifers on The Chains, unspoiled moorland which belonged to Lord Fortescue. They were already acquainted with the Barnstaple doctor, Richard 'Dick' Harper, and his wife Margery, who were organising opposition. In June a meeting took place between the Chairman of the National Parks Commission, the Chairman of the Forestry Commission and Lord Fortescue, during which the intensity of local feeling against the proposal was discussed. Shortly after this, Lord Fortescue and his wife died within days of each other.

Mary says that Brian felt guilty that he had indirectly contributed to Lord Fortescue's death, though in his article in Volume 39 of the Exmoor Review he writes: 'I respected the Earl as landowner and had not seen myself lecturing him on the management of his property. Now it suddenly looked as if the time to do something had arrived.'

The opposition campaign stepped up with letters to the local, regional and national press, followed by a petition started by Dr Harper, co-sponsored by the Misses Enid and Maud Milman of Swimbridge, who had been Land Girls in the First World War, ran a small farm and were stalwart moor walkers. They were joined by a relative of the Milmans, Miss Margery Oldham, who lived near Dunkery. The petition was launched in August and Mary describes how she asked everyone she knew for signatures. 'I was 23 and completely naïve about political matters,' she says ruefully. 'But it was rather easier in those days to make contact with people. North Devon seemed smaller somehow.'

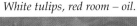
White tulips, red room – oil.

They were still collecting signatures when the official announcement came on 27 November that the afforestation proposal had been withdrawn.

Meanwhile, many of those who had petitioned against afforestation came together with Major John Coleman-Cooke, Victor Bonham-Carter, Tim Burton, John Goodland and others to form the Exmoor Society. 'It was a very small affair to begin with,' Mary explains, 'but after the success of the Petition it was realised that we needed "a watch-dog", a society that would keep an eye on what was happening on the moor in order to preserve its unique character and wilderness.'

Monet's lake at Giverny – acrylics.

Since then, Mary has twice been presented with the Founder's Award. The first time was with Brian in 1985 in recognition of the part played by them and Margery Harper in the launching of the Petition. The second occasion was in 2011, in recognition of her 'immense contribution' to the Society, especially its work with children, her chairman-ship of the Barnstaple Group and her significant contribution to the Society's Education Endowment Fund.

Since Brian has dominated so much of our conversation, I am wondering if Mary had suffered any creative block after his death. 'No,' she said, 'rather the opposite. I think my tears went into the water colours which I did at that time. I was greatly helped by my friends, of all ages, and I went for many long walks on Exmoor and the coastal

path – on my own as I needed to think about the "seismic shift" that had taken place in my life.'

She leads the way to her workroom, where the walls are covered with her paintings – views, people, birds, flowers. They have an ethereal quality all of their own, as if you are looking at the subjects through a translucent layer, that pulls you into it as you try to get a clearer view.

Does she have a preferred medium? I ask, aware of the mundanity of my question. 'No, I use oils, acrylics, water colour, mixed media and, recently, pastels.' And where do her ideas come from? 'All directions – from my imagination, places seen, incidents experienced, people, situations and often ideas just arrive on the ether.' Last year she visited Monet's Garden at Giverny and she is currently attending life-drawing sessions. Several times a year, she joins a group of friends for a ladies' lunch at each other's homes. All of these things have inspired some of her more recent paintings featured in her summer 2013 exhibition at the Plough Arts Centre, Torrington.

'I am enjoying my seventies,' Mary says. 'Once you are turned seventy, you know yourself quite well and if one is fortunate in having good health, good friends and time to contemplate and observe this remarkable planet which we inhabit, then these are riches indeed.'

Farming and Fiction
Victoria Eveleigh

Chris and Victoria Eveleigh.
PHOTO BY GUY HARROP

2013 has been a busy year for children's author Victoria Eveleigh, as her new trilogy is published by Orion Children's Books: Joe and the Hidden Horseshoe, Joe and the Lightning Pony and Joe and the Race to Rescue. Jenny Gibson asked her to tell us how she came to be a writer and where she finds her ideas.

Were you born and raised on Exmoor? If not, what brought you here?

I was born and raised in London, but my grandmother owned West Ilkerton Farm, near Lynton, and I used to stay with her whenever I could in the school holidays. To me Exmoor was paradise. By the time I was a teenager I'd decided I wanted to marry a farmer and live on Exmoor – and somehow I've managed to do both!

After university I moved to Exmoor, lived at the farm and worked part-time for the Exmoor National Park Authority. Before long I'd met a handsome young farm manager called Chris Eveleigh. We were soon married, and we've been running the farm for 27 years now. Chris was born at Parsonage Farm, Bratton Fleming, so he's Exmoor born and bred even if I'm not.

Your books are about horses and ponies. Why do you write pony stories?

I've always loved ponies. One of my earliest memories is the rag-and-bone man's pony that regularly visited our street in London (that dates me!) and learning to ride on the sand tracks around Hyde Park. When I stayed with Grandma on Exmoor I learned how to ride 'properly' across real countryside with Helen Bingham at Outovercott Riding Stables. My favourite treat was helping to ride and lead the Outovercott horses to Brendon to be shod in Fred Kent's forge.

I wasn't particularly keen on reading when I was a child, but pony books were the exception that proved the rule. I loved stories by Primrose Cumming, Pat Smyth, K.M. Peyton and Monica Dickens and, of course, *Moorland Mousie* by Golden Gorse.

I started writing pony stories mainly because I was appalled by *My Little Pony* and the other unrealistic 'pink' pony stories that were available when our daughter Sarah was a girl. I longed to write the sort of thing I'd enjoyed as a child. A story formed in my mind about a girl and a pony growing up together on an Exmoor farm – inspired by Sarah and her feisty Exmoor pony, Frithelsden Tinkerbell (Tinks for short) and our experiences of farming on Exmoor and keeping a herd of free-living Exmoor ponies.

Have you always been a writer?
No. Not in the sense that it's been a job, anyway. I've always enjoyed writing stories, and letters were an important part of my childhood because I went to boarding school.

Unlike most authors, I gave up studying English after O Levels, and studied Geography at university followed by an MSc in Agricultural Economics. When I was working for the Exmoor National Park Authority we produced a series of walks leaflets and educational leaflets for schools. A lot of the things I learned then I used when publishing my own books.

When did you write your first book?
I wrote my first story about Katy and her Exmoor pony, Trifle, in 2001. The foot and mouth crisis during that year meant that normal life was put on hold and I had the opportunity to sit down and write. I sent the story to several agents and received rejec-

Some of the West Ilkerton Exmoors.

tions from all of them. However, friends and family encouraged me to publish the story myself. The book sold amazingly well in local shops, so I wrote another, and another …

How many books have you written now?
There'll be seven by the end of 2013, or eight if you count *The Exmoor Horn Colouring Book,* which Chris and I did for the Exmoor Horn Sheep Breeders' Society. The books are *Katy's Wild Foal, Katy's Champion Pony, Katy's Pony Surprise, A Stallion Called Midnight, Joe and the Hidden Horseshoe, Joe and the Lightning Pony* and *Joe and the Race to Rescue.*

How did you get them published?
Initially I published the Katy books and the one about Midnight myself (under the titles *Katy's Exmoor, Katy's Exmoor Adventures, Katy's Exmoor Friends* and *Midnight on Lundy*). However, in 2011 I was taken on by a major publishing house, Orion, and was asked to rewrite my existing books (under new titles) and write a completely new trilogy as well.

'Orion the Exmoor Pony – I named our only Exmoor colt foal Orion because I was so thrilled that Orion Children's Books were going to publish my stories.'

How did you feel when Orion asked to publish you?
It took a while to sink in, but I was delighted. It's a real treat to have two editors to guide me, proof readers, marketing managers, a publicist and so on. I've learned a huge amount about writing and the book industry since I've been writing for Orion. It's lovely to make friends with fellow authors too.

I love the drawings by your husband, Chris.
I love Chris' drawings as well. When our children were young, Chris told them stories about Grandpa's farm and a fictional character on our farm called the Old Man of Marleycombe, and he drew lots of pictures to go with the stories, so Chris was the natural illustrator for my books. We were both delighted when Orion took him on as the illustrator for my books.

Are any of the characters in your books based on real people or animals?
I get ideas for aspects of human characters from real life, of course, but it's always dangerous to take a complete, recognisable person and plonk him or her into a book. Apart from anything else, an author can never know a real character as completely as they have to know their fictional creations.

Orion in the snow.

The horses in my books are fictional as well, but some of them were strongly influenced by real horses and ponies.

Jacko in the Katy books is the only pony I've taken from real life more-or-less unchanged. He was my first pony, and I loved him dearly.

Midnight in *A Stallion Called Midnight* is also based on a real pony, but I never knew him. I found out what he was like from people who'd known him on Lundy in the 1950s and '60s, and from Peggy Garvey who bought him after he was shipped to the mainland. I was delighted when Peggy told me my portrayal of Midnight was spot on.

Trifle in the Katy books was based on Sarah's pony Tinks and an Exmoor pony called Twiggy that I used to ride as a child.

I got the idea for Lightning in the Horseshoe trilogy from a games pony called Danny, owned by the Capel family from Wootton Courtenay, and Sherman in *Joe and the Race to Rescue* was inspired by our lovely Shire horse, although the fictional Sherman is dappled grey rather than black because it made a better cover picture.

And I named our only Exmoor colt foal Orion because I was so thrilled that Orion Children's books were going to publish my stories.

Your first books all had girls as the central characters. What made you change to a boy for your latest trilogy?

There are girls in the *Horseshoe* trilogy, but I wanted to make the central character a boy because there aren't many modern British pony stories with strong boy characters in them – in fact, I can only think of a couple of excellent stories for young adults by Sheena Wilkinson called *Taking Flight* and *Grounded*.

There are plenty of boys who ride and are interested in horses but they seem to have been marginalised due to the 'pink pony culture' that seems to prevail in children's literature nowadays.

It was quite a challenge to think like a boy when I was writing this trilogy. Joe is very different from Katy in the *Katy's Ponies* trilogy or Jenny in *A Stallion Called Midnight*.

None of my books are specifically for boys or girls. I have tried to make sure all of them feature strong characters of both sexes. I think stories with both boys and girls in them are much more interesting – like a party where everyone's invited.

Further information about Victoria and her books can be found on her website www.victoriaeveleigh.co.uk and you can follow her on Facebook (Victoria Eveleigh Author) and Twitter (@TortieEveleigh). Her books are available from bookshops, online stores and several gift shops on Exmoor. Anyone wanting to purchase the books wholesale should contact The Orion Publishing Group on 020 7240 3444 and ask to speak to Sales.

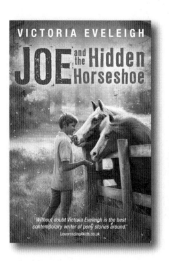
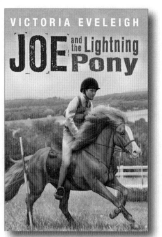
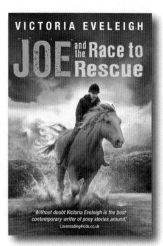

Jenny Gibson has written five novels, published in the UK and in translation, under the name Jenny Glanfield. Some of her father's family farmed for several generations on Exmoor and in 2002 she moved from Kent to re-establish her roots in her spiritual home.

COASTAL EXMOOR

Adrian Tierney-Jones

I must go down to the seas again, to the lonely sea and the sky…

There's something about a coastal landscape, its sights, signs and sounds, that for me always leads to poetry. If it's not John Masefield's masterly *Sea Fever* that springs to mind, it's Matthew Arnold's *Dover Beach* with its evocation of *'the grating roar/ Of pebbles which the waves draw back, and fling/ At their return, up the high strand,/ Begin, and cease, and then again begin,/ With tremulous cadence slow, and bring/ The eternal note of sadness in'.* There is a massive sense of yearning and poignancy about the sea and the coast, something deep that cannot be easily explained – and the Exmoor coastline has a pull on my emotions as much as did the North Wales coast alongside which I grew up.

It's a place for discovery, which is what I often do: discover. Take Minehead beach, beyond the harbour, at a point where the South West Coastal Path starts its climb towards Selworthy Beacon; here it seems to me that the Exmoor coast returns to its

Greenaleigh

natural sense of wildness as it leaves behind the fun-of-the-fair lightness of the town and the long history of maritime commerce that has defined Minehead, Dunster and Watchet. It's almost as if the coast is a living thing and that it dares to draw breath once more and express its true elemental state – and on a cold spring day earlier this year I began my latest discovery, leaping from stone to stone on the rocky beach, with Hurlstone Point and its conjoined twin Porlock Bay as my ultimate goal.

The waters of the Bristol Channel were quiet on this day, as if tired and restful after their recent stormy interludes, the evidence of which was scattered at the high water mark – the relics of trees, both branches and whole logs, lay still, some of them as white and bleached as the most weathered bone. Elsewhere more of the detritus of the sea lay about, a splattering of rubbish: over there a massive orange-coloured Wellington boot, here some netting, and close by a tangle of eviscerated rope. Hidden away, half buried in a patch of sand, was the axle of a tractor, battered and bruised by the weather. Did the latter piece of junk come from the land above, where the cliffs rise, Devonian stone and slate, modest at first, though still treacherous enough for the casual scrambler? Landslides had occurred; trees had skidded down and exposed the red soil and rock to the light. Looking at a raw, stubbly, crumbling slope of stones, soil and small pathetic patches of grass it would be easy to think of nature at its most violent. However, here I think it's more of a case of nature shrugging its shoulders and letting a landslide happen, almost casual, rather than a burst of explosive rage.

Seagulls patrolled the edge of the water, seemingly held stationary by the air currents, reminiscent of the description of a scene from Daphne Du Maurier's *The Birds*, though the squadrons of gulls in this classic avian chiller were a lot more sinister in their intention as they waited for the tide to turn and the time to attack humanity. And as if to expel all thoughts of the viciousness of *The Birds*, there was the sound of the gulls, staccato screeches reminiscent of some strange jazz ensemble. And while the gulls uttered their wails and crakes, the susurration of the waves added a softer, more benevolent background.

When we think about Exmoor and explain its attractions to those who know little of the place I believe that there is often the temptation to forget about the coastline and its beauty. Exmoor? we are asked. It's a land of heather, bracken, red deer, sheep and ponies comes the reply, all happily co-existing on the high moors or in the beautiful little valleys that cut through the land. However, it is also a land of high sea cliffs through which cut steep-sided combes stitched with a rich green tapestry of broad-leaved trees, some of them families of ancient oaks standing sentinel; there are also the lonely coves and storm-battered beaches like the one west of Minehead. The Exmoor National Park gives the length of the coastline as 34 miles; it also estimates that 'if you were to wait for tides low enough to walk between access points it would take five years to walk the 34 mile length of shore. Even then some serious rock climbing would be involved.' (http://www.exmoor-nationalpark.gov.uk/learning/did-you-know)

There are many faces to the Exmoor coastline. It's hardy, rough-coated, but also beautiful; it's playful and yet artful in the way it can turn the tables on the casual explorer, as

I discovered on my walk. The tide was out when I left, but after two hours of painful perambulation along the large pebbles and stones that litter the beach, the wide golden sands of Selworthy Beach beckoned. My feet had a respite and I was able to walk without looking at the ground, able to take in the expanse of sand and the steepness of the cliffs rising upwards to Selworthy Beacon. Hurlstone Point lay ahead and beyond it the shelter of Porlock Bay (the wind was north-easterly and bracing in its effect). The tide had turned though, and was coming in fast. By the time I reached the Point the sand was vanishing beneath the sea and I was forced to climb onto a slightly sloping rock platform and then progress through a hole in the rock through whose end I overlooked the Bay. I was through but for a moment it looked as if I might need to plunge into water to get round. Fortunately I didn't and after some clambering and skidding across rock I was safe on the loose collection of stones that makes up Porlock Bay.

There is more to this coastal musing than one – long, stone-strewn – beach though. Further west past Porlock Weir, the cliffs soar and sing in their zeal to reach the heavens. From here onwards, the traveller can experience some of the highest sea cliffs in the UK. The woodland continues to carpet the land, some of it reaching down as the shore's edge; it is a place through which the red deer creep, ghostly in their shadowy presence. As streams and rivers urgently rush down towards the sea, you might see a dipper hopping, skipping and jumping, while the odd yellow wagtail struts about, comical and slightly skittish, a neurotic kind of bird; above in the sky a raven will be drifting on the aerials or – if you are lucky as I was – a peregrine falcon.

I love the Exmoor coastline, whether it's a battered beach, a soaring cliff-top that reminds me of the heights of my native North Wales, the long vista across the battleship grey waters of the Bristol Channel or the magical crevices in which hide the likes of Combe Martin or Lynmouth. The latter place feels like Brigadoon, possibly only visible on a certain night of the year. It's a place that seems on the edge of the world, secure, secluded, a fortress-like village that can only be approached over the heights, down a windy road, through the arboreal guardians of woodland and forest.

Yet coastal Exmoor can also have its dark side. I remember the story of a car that came off the road east of Lynmouth and plunged down the side of the slope; boats have been wrecked against the cliffs though many others have been rescued; while Lynmouth famously and tragically endured its own Calvary in 1952 when heavy rain on the moor created a perfect storm drain of destruction. But let us not dwell on the dark; there is plenty of light on the coast of Exmoor.

I must go down to the seas again, to the lonely sea and the sky...

Adrian Tierney-Jones is an award-winning freelance journalist based in Dulverton whose work appears in the *Daily Telegraph* (regular pub reviews and features on the countryside page), and in many other publications.

Looking across Porlock Bay to Hurlstone Point.

TREASURING EXMOOR'S TREES

John Wibberley

Trees are vital to earth's ecosystem. In many places, loss of trees is faster than replacement. Trees are a multi-faceted source of wealth, as well as for carbon sequestration in these global-warming conscious days. Not just foresters and forest communities but also civil societies, families and individuals at large need to care about and for trees.

Globally, forests cover some 3.9 billion hectares (9.6 billion acres) which is approximately 30% of the world's land surface. The UN Food & Agriculture Organisation (FAO, 2012) estimates that around 13 million hectares of forests were converted to other uses or lost through natural causes annually between 2000 and 2010. Their estimated annual rate of forest area increase was 5 million hectares.

Trees should be valued at various levels – intrinsically as God's creation, as notable specimens and as landscape features, for their products, for their protection and for their global ecosystem role.

Trees are treasured by some as ethical investments, where *Ethical Forestry* (www.ethicalforestry.com) cites a *Moneyweek* claim 'forestry is the only asset class in existence that has risen in three out of the four market collapses of the 20th century'. Timber is uncorrelated to stock markets with almost sixfold investment growth projected over 12 years. Trees have benefited from the dedicated attention of enthusiasts, such as Michael Heathcoat Amory's remarkable and comprehensive collection of oaks (*Quercus* spp.) begun at Chevithorne Barton in the Exe Valley approaches to Exmoor in 1984, and now the largest such collection in the UK, and probably globally (Heathcoat Amory, 2009). Trees ultimately exemplify God's good creation. Substantial healing now is possible using knowledge of the healing properties of various trees. The spiritual significance of trees perhaps relates in part to the fact that many of them and their associated forests far transcend the span of a human life. It is said of the English oak that it takes 300 years to grow, lives 300 years and takes 300 years to die! The tallest tree in England is in Dunster Forest, Exmoor – a Douglas fir (*Pseudotsuga menziesii*) at over 60m.

The UK has only 5 ha of forest per 100 population by contrast with the world average of 60 hectares. However, Exmoor not only has a higher proportion of woodland at 13.5% cover than the rest of England (barely 10%), but also 91 ha per 100 of its resident population. Graeme McVittie, Exmoor's Woodlands Officer, estimates that the proportions of different types of woodland within Exmoor National Park are as shown in the table below.

CONIFER PLANTATIONS	32%	MIXED	5%
BROADLEAF SECONDARY	29%	SCRUB	10%
BROADLEAF ANCIENT & S-N*	24%	*S-N = semi-natural	

It is perhaps ironic that the origins of the *Exmoor Society* in 1958 were not the crass removal of trees from Exmoor – which might have instigated conservation societies elsewhere – but rather the Forestry Commission's proposed planting of serried ranks of conifers across the open moorland of The Chains!

The medieval Royal Forest of Exmoor centred on Simonsbath and was under the jurisdiction of the agents of successive monarchs as a hunting area, expanding to its peak under Henry III's 1217 Charter of Forests. The ENPA field guide to this area is concisely informative (Siraut, 2013).

Hinde (1985) cites three notable landowners who have left their marks on the Royal Forest:

James Boevey (17th C) made Simonsbath the Forest centre; planted the Hoar Oak tree; Thomas Acland (18th C) as careful custodian of the Forest, re-established stag hunting; John Knight (19th C) by draining, farms/field demarcation with mainly beech hedging.

These beech hedges have now become iconic symbols of the Exmoor that is treasured today. It is vital that means are found to maintain all of them as the ESA (Environmentally Sensitive Areas) grant schemes are replaced by HLS & UEL (Higher

Tarr Steps

Level Stewardship & Upland Entry Level schemes). Farm shelterbelts were often planted for protection in these windswept uplands, also providing a ready supply of fuelwood and farmstead construction timber. Scots pine trees were planted as 'nurse' trees in the establishment of these shelterbelts, while alder was used in the same way in wetter areas. Notable plantations of holm oak (*Quercus ilex*) thrive north of Bossington where this species favours the sea air as elsewhere in the south-west of England. Among the ancient oaks of Exmoor are those near Porlock, and perhaps most notably those of Horner Wood near Dunkery, which Burton (1978) tells us derives its name from *hwrnwr* 'the snorer', referring to the violent sound of its stream in spate! Horner Wood is regarded as Exmoor's most ancient wood as reflected in the rich biodiversity within it, though chiefly comprised of oaks (notably gnarled *Quercus robur*), ash (*Fraxinus excelsior*) and the splendidly 'coppicing-suited' hazel (*Corylus avellana*). Culbone Wood seems to have been at the centre of Exmoor's charcoal burning industry. Notable conifers within Exmoor include not only larch (*Larix* spp.) but also Douglas fir (*Pseudotsuga* spp.), which latter eminently suits the south-west climate and produces elegant timber for flooring and other construction work. A still most useful authoritative survey of Exmoor's trees and woods is that of Miles (1972). We are blessed with iconic wooded Exmoor heritage, though it cost over £100,000 to clear the trees damaged and falling into over-silted watercourses during the storms of January 2013.

The Green Belt Movement (GBM) was begun in 1977 in Kenya by the late Wangari Maathai (2006) – though she began with her own small tree nursery in 1974. Engaging local farmers is key. GBM bases its work on the following values:- love for environment conservation; self and community empowerment; volunteerism; strong sense of belonging to a community of like-minded people; accountability; transparency; and honesty.

GBM results have been spectacular, with well over 30 million trees planted in Kenya alone. Rural employment has been created and environmental awareness raised. Individuals and communities have been inspired, empowered and mobilised. Biodiversity, a wider range of food crops and water catchments, have been protected locally.

That trees and forests need management is beyond doubt and coppicing can provide regular harvests. Community forestry can engage all ages of people both in new communal plantations and in managing indigenous ancient forests. The human dimensions of deforestation need better understanding and action too. While forest protection is imperative as are reduced emissions from deforestation and desertification (REDD), exclusion of indigenous people from forests for the benefit of tourism and extractive business elites is a travesty. So also is the granting of carbon credits for forest protection to poorer countries if it is done so that the richer countries providing it can continue to behave unsustainably with their own forests! Long-term sustainable management and public enjoyment of forests cannot be attained unless indigenous populations and their livelihoods are recognised and mobilised to care. This occurred successfully through England's only rural development forestry initiative, The South-West (Thomas & Wibberley, 2001). It should be revived and rolled out. Those who plant their own trees tend to care for them. Only by engaging local people and integrating tree care within their livelihoods can progress be attained. This will be vital in 'unlocking the potential of Exmoor's Woodlands' (Jones & Vaughan, 2013). Exmoor's tree treasure is immense and could be better harnessed – the beauty of truly renewable resources!

References & Further Reading

Blyth, J., Evans, J., Mutch, W.E.S. & Sidwell, C. (1987) *Farm Woodland Management.* (Farming Press, UK & USA, 189 pp.).

Bonham Carter, V. (1991) *The Essence of Exmoor* – notably Ch.5 pp.62-79 *Trees.* (Exmoor Press, Dulverton, 200 pp.).

Burton, S.H. (1978, 3rd edn.) *Exmoor.* (Robert Hale, London, 192 pp.).

FAO (2011) *State of the World's Forests.* (9th biennial edn., FAO, Rome).

Forsyth, T. & Sikor, T. (2013) Forests, development and the globalisation of justice. *The Geographical Journal*, **179 (2)** 114-121.

Giono, J. (1954 – 11th impr. 2000). *The Man Who Planted Trees.*(P. Owen, London, 52 pp.).

Heathcoat Amory, M. (2009) *The Oaks of Chevithorne Barton.* (Adelphi Publ., London, 219 pp.).

Hinde, T. (1985) *Forests of Britain.* (Abacus, London, 349 pp.).

Jones, L. & Vaughan, S. (2013) Unlocking the potential of Exmoor's Woodlands. (Report to Exmoor Society and partners, in press).

Maathai, W.M.(2006) – 1st edn 1995. *The Greenbelt Movement.* (Lantern Bks, NY, 138pp).

Macpherson, G. (1995) *Home-grown Energy from short-rotation Coppice.* (Farming Press, UK & USA, 214 pp.).

McMahon, P. (2009) *Rain Forests: the burning issue.*(The Prince's Rainforests Trust, 48 pp).

Miles, R. (1972) *Trees & Woods of Exmoor.* (Exmoor Press, Dulverton, 64pp.).

Siraut, M. (2013) *A Field Guide to The Royal Forest of Exmoor.* (ENPA, 20pp.).

Thomas, R. & Wibberley, E.J. (2001) Integrated Rural Development: Agriculture & Rural Development Forestry. *Journal of the Royal Agricultural Society of England*, **162**, 89-96. (www.rase.org.uk).

Wibberley, E.J. (2013) Treasuring Trees for Agricultural Transformation. IFMA19 (International Farm Management Association 19th congress, Poland, July 2013 (in press).

Wood, P.J. & Burley, J. (1991) *A Tree for all Reasons.* (ICRAF, Nairobi, 158 pp.).

Professor John Wibberley PhD, FRAgS, FRGS works internationally in agriculture and rural resource management, especially in the UK and Africa. He co-ordinates the UK Council for Awards of Royal Agricultural Societies, which seeks to recognise outstanding contributions to agricultural and rural progress within the UK, and he serves as a Secretary of State appointee for Exmoor National Park.

FORESTS

Martin Hesp

Forests are the stuff of life. Without them we wouldn't be here. They give us much of the oxygen we breathe – they soak up much of the carbon we emit. And they are our ancient home. Once, not so very long ago, the great majority of mankind lived in forests.

Now we pillage them. We chop and burn vast acreages. We annihilate rainforest so we can grow palm oil. Even our own politicians seem to think so little of forests they'd have sold our publicly owned woodlands if there hadn't been a public revolt. Perhaps the politicians had overlooked a silent but powerful force that lies deep within most people – an inherent love of trees and of the haunting, magical, qualities of forested landscapes.

Forests might be good for our mental and physical wellbeing (as has been proved in research projects in countries like Sweden, South Korea and Japan); they might be beneficial in helping raise natural biodiversity; and they might be natural and beautiful carbon sinks that help us fight climate change… But it is difficult to imagine a UK government which was hell-bent on selling forests suddenly deciding to invest in trees and plant more.

The growing number of hard working woodland volunteers gives us one reason to be optimistic about a future for this region's trees – but here's another. A few months ago a new report by the Forestry Commission revealed that the South West of England has 22 per cent more forest than previously known, increasing the total area by 45,030 hectares to 251,638 hectares.

It means that more than 11 per cent of our landscapes are covered in woodlands – the assumed figure previously stood at just under nine per cent tree-cover. The increase has come to light thanks to a greater accuracy in research techniques – modern aerial camera and mapping equipment is able to detect many more smaller broadleaf forests than was the case when the last census report was published in 1998.

Last year the Exmoor Society, in partnership with the Exmoor National Park Authority, staged an important conference in a bid to look at future potential for local woodlands and "demystify" the complex issues involved in managing them. It was Simon Hodgson, chief executive of the Forestry Commission, who told delegates about the nation's embarrassingly treeless status, declaring that England was a "very unwooded country". With such a small resource of forested landscape this country, he said, was the fourth largest importer of timber in the world.

The national park authority's woodland officer, Graeme McVittie, outlined the variety of forest-types that were to be found in the region, stating that Exmoor boasts an "unrivalled history and diversity of trees and woodlands". He said: "The coastal woodlands which extend to the shoreline in places are unique in the region and Exmoor has a significant proportion of the UK and world total of the remaining western sessile oak woods."

However, not everything was serene in the sylvan acres of the national park's woodlands... Exmoor Society chairman Rachel Thomas set a challenge for the National Park Authority by saying its new management plan lacked a "coherent framework". She said "each worthwhile project mentioned" in the plans appeared "unconnected and piecemeal".

This may well be correct, but after making extensive travels around the woodlands of the West Country peninsula in order to write three separate newspaper series and many other individual articles about our forests, it is to the magical tree-cover of Exmoor that I turn if I want to see the most superior sylvan sights of them all. Even in cold December rain Horner Woods somehow looks like, and probably is, the nearest thing England has to natural, unspoilt, primary rainforest.

The woodland is of national and international importance with particular nature conservation interest in its lichen (330 species), fungi, bryophyte and bats (15 species) and lowland heath. That a single wood – here in over-busy, over-developed, Southern England – could boast 330 different types of anything is amazing – but those teeming lichens make Horner Woods one of the richest such places in all of Europe. We can thank the clear, unpolluted Atlantic air that washes through the complex of combes for this particular treasure trove – lichens do not like even the slightest dose of mankind's atmospheric filth and could not survive in locations closer to our more populated areas.

Horner Woods are billed as "one of the largest single areas of unenclosed ancient semi-natural woodland in England". That term "ancient semi-natural woodland" might seem to be an anathema – for a start, the word "ancient" could lead you to think this is what much of Southern England would have looked like before mankind turned up and started clearing forest for his farmsteads. Well, yes – and no. The indigenous trees would certainly have dominated things, but the woodlands would probably have been a good deal more thicketed – and this is where the "semi-natural" phrase has relevance.

Horner Woods have been worked by mankind for centuries, right up until the early 1920s. People lived and laboured in the woods producing tan bark for the leather industry and, of course, charcoal and timber. In order for them to be productive the woods were coppiced and pollarded – cut back in various ways and allowed to grow new shoots – a type of management that opened up the forest and prevented it from becoming dark and choked with thicket.

This work of yesteryear still has echoes in the way the woods look today. A recent survey to assess the number and condition of Horner's ancient trees showed that the wood contains 1039 veterans of which 478 are pollards. Now the National Trust is working to maintain this "semi-natural" status of the forest.

It's an illustration which shows us that managing our trees and woodlands has always been a balancing act. Cut and burn too much and you tip the scales – plant vast acreages with mono-crops of pines and you upset the equilibrium another way. It is a woodland balancing act I have written about in a Western Morning News series called the Contested Landscape in which I tracked the recent history of what I journalistically described as tree-wars. The biggest row of all occurred in the early 1900s when the trend was for coniferous planting on an industrial scale.

At first this was done without protest, but eventually the nation was to turn against the concept of block-planting vast areas with fast growing pines. An area of Devon just a few miles south of Exmoor happens to be the very first place where the newly formed Forestry Commission swung into conifer-planting action. It was 94 years ago, on 8 December 1919, that Lord Clinton, a newly appointed Forestry Commission commissioner, planted some Douglas firs on his Eggesford estate.

The First World War had just ended and the mass-planting of forests was deemed both necessary and patriotic. The great conflict had lain bare the nation's frailty when it came to just about anything which had to be imported, and it was realised we needed to grow as much of our own timber as possible. And we needed to do it fast – hence the quick growing conifers.

A couple of decades later the next great war doubly underlined this requirement - and still the zealous tree-planting sense of patriotism far outstripped any concerns for the environment. Large conifer plantations were the result – and they were located in the more remote wilderness areas like Exmoor. Prime agricultural land was never going to be given over to a crop that took at least 50 years to mature, so it was the marginal areas like the high moors that tended to play host to rank upon rank of dark conifers. Some of these forests still stand, although they are managed in a different way.

But the fact is we'd have inherited far more of these vast plantations if people hadn't started ringing alarm bells in the 1960s and '70s. The first of those protestors were to be found here on Exmoor. Over half a century ago the Forestry Commission had plans for a truly massive planting on The Chains area – and the Exmoor Society came into being as a result of fighting that battle.

So much for the wooded battles of the past – but are commercial forests still a contested landscape? If they're not, then does environmentally friendly forestry have a place in times when hard economics must drive all? If so, could we see a more forested landscape in the future?

These fairly bald questions have fascinating answers – as I have discovered while interviewing arboricultural experts across the peninsula. For a start, we still need timber but for decades we seem to have been happy to import vast amounts of it.

"The market for timber evolves," I was told by one forest manager. "Old markets disappear and new ones come along – but the market in this country for timber is huge. We each consume the equivalent of a tonne of timber a year but domestically we only produce about eight or nine million tonnes. The rest is all imported. In fact, there are only three things that cost this country more in terms of imports - that's fuel, food and motor vehicles.

"If we want to sell our timber to processors, it has to compete with price of imported timber. That limits what we can do at the moment. But I'm sure our time will come - when we are not just paying the economic value, but also for the environmental value of our goods."

Another forestry expert told me: "The amount of timber we import could plummet and the amount of domestic timber could increase significantly. We have to discuss more openly the politics of taking dubiously controlled amounts of timber from rainforests, not to mention the price of hauling such a bulk commodity halfway around the planet."

So, could a "grow-your-own" strategy see a return to the days of mass-block-planting? According to experts I've interviewed, that is simply not the modern forester's way. Contemporary practice relies on a system of thinning – much of the young material that comes out of the woods gets made into wood chips or other processed material. Progressively, as the trees that are left grow bigger, the next round of thinning will go in to things like fence panels, cable drums, pallets and so on. Eventually, the forest grows on to provide the larger diameter material – logs that are big enough for proper timber usage.

There could be another future benefit if the subject of climate change moves up a gear… "The 16,000 hectares of forest which I'm responsible for in the South West lock up around 33,000 tonnes of carbon a year," I was told by one Forestry Commission manager. "And that's on top of producing 90,000 tonnes of timber sustainably, alongside providing all those other benefits like access and wildlife habitats.

"To my mind, the forest is one of the habitats of the future – it is robust, it is capable of delivering huge benefits – and here in the South West we've hardly scratched the surface."

It is difficult to argue with that kind of enthusiasm. Perhaps the woodlands of Exmoor – both and ancient and modern – do have a future.

Martin has been a professional journalist for 35 years, working for newspapers, magazines, radio and TV. Now editor-at-large at *Western Morning News*, he travels the South West peninsula looking for good stories. He has also written one novel *The Last Broomsquire*.

SIMONSBATH FESTIVAL 2013

Victoria Thomas

Simonsbath Festival is definitely finding a place on the cultural map of Exmoor, settling into its six-week slot in the spring calendar between May Day and Midsummer. After the successful first festival last year, support from the local community and beyond encouraged us to plan a second festival with an even bigger variety of concerts, events and activities. Through word of mouth and social media, as well as a growing database of email addresses, attendance was significantly higher. And a real boost this year was a £6,000 award from the Heritage Lottery Fund to revive the traditional music and songs of Exmoor.

With its unique setting in the tiny, remote village of Simonsbath in the heart of Exmoor, the festival is finding its own unique character – essential in a crowded marketplace where the English summer is positively teeming with festivals of one sort of another. The central idea is to celebrate the cultural heritage of Exmoor, with traditional May Day and Midsummer festivities to open and close the festival, while inviting musicians from abroad to celebrate their cultural heritage. Another aim is to fit as much variety – and as many surprises – as possible into the programme so that it reflects the rich variety of life.

For us, one of the big surprises from the first year was that the world music events attracted more interest than the traditional May Day and Midsummer celebrations of Exmoor's own cultural heritage. A reason seemed to be a lack of awareness in the community of local folk heritage and traditions, so we set out to redress the balance looking to the folk and community arts organisation Wren Music with their project 'Songs from the Exmoor Forest'. This involved co-founders Marilyn Tucker and Paul Wilson giving concerts and running workshops to teach the folk music, songs and traditions collected in Exmoor Forest from the early 20th century to the 1980s. This included material collected by Cecil Sharp, who noted nearly 3,300 songs in England, more than 100 of these being gathered from Exmoor. The other main body of work was Paul Wilson's collection of folk songs from his visits to Exmoor in the 1970s, following in Cecil Sharp's footsteps across the moor.

At a concert which was part of the May Day celebrations, including children's maypole dancing, an art workshop and storytelling, we heard a version of 'Van Dieman's Land' which was collected from Exford in 1906 from Robert Parish, one of the main contributors to Cecil Sharp's Exmoor collection. The song tells of the harsh penalties meted out for petty crimes, often involving deportation to the penal colony on the island of Tasmania, off southern Australia, which used to be known as Van Dieman's Land.

There was also a series of weekly evening workshops for anyone interested, along with workshops for children at local schools, all culminating in a Midsummer concert at St

Luke's to mark the end of the festival, in which local residents and invited guests, including Voices in Common North Devon folk choir, Martyn Babb and children from Dulverton and Exford schools all joined. If Simonsbath Festival does establish itself as an annual event, the aim is to provide a platform for the performance of Songs from the Exmoor Forest for years to come. The idea of bringing as much variety as possible into the mix of festival events has proved a popular one. Thus we enjoyed a concert by promising young opera singers, closely followed by a celebration of farming communities from the 1920s to 1970s.

Another venue, the historic sawmill, hosted a series of talks by local experts entitled *The Secrets of Simonsbath* about the cultural and historical heritage of the area which were accompanied by short walks to relevant sites.

In contrast, the Exmoor Forest Inn hosted a Gumboot Dance workshop about a tradition which originated in the gold mines of South Africa. Workshop tutor Cecilia Ndhlovu taught adults and children a whole new language, dance and culture based on that most humble and yet – to many Exmoor residents and visitors – most indispensable piece of footwear: the wellington boot. In South African gold mines miners were forbidden to talk so they created their own means of communication to keep up morale. The Gumboot Dance is now recognised nationally as a South African traditional dance and celebrated today to mark the end of slavery in the mines.

The festival was originally inspired by the restoration of St Luke's Church, and built on the success of the concerts held there to raise money towards the £300,000 restoration project. The attractive interior and outstanding acoustics that have made St Luke's a popular venue for amateur and professional concerts are also ideal for the festival and work continues to add versatility and functionality to the church. Last year the Bath and Wells Diocese Fund for Church Growth awarded a grant of up to £2,000 for the installation of a sound system in recognition of the role of the festival in the future of St Luke's in partnership with the wider community. The festival now has to look for ways to find match funding from this year's proceeds and other sources.

Another welcome addition to St Luke's was made by Robin Ashburner's construction of huge black-out blinds for the church's stained glass windows, so that films can be screened. The plan is to include more of these next year, and to add films to the other fund-raising events held in St Luke's throughout the year.

If you would like to help in the organisation of the festival, make a donation, become a Friend of Simonsbath Festival or join the mailing list, please contact Victoria Thomas on 01643 831343 or email simonsbathfestival@mail.com. You can follow the festival on Facebook and Twitter and visit the website at www.simonsbathfestival.co.uk

Victoria's family is from north Devon and, although born in Malaysia, she has known and loved Exmoor all her life, where she has now lived for 23 years. Inspired by the restoration of St Luke's, in 2012 Victoria founded Simonsbath Festival which she now chairs.

A Visit to Ash Farm, Culbone –
in the Footsteps of Coleridge

Mark Haworth-Booth

Ash Farm, nestled among the sloping fields above Culbone Church, is generally agreed to be the place where Samuel Taylor Coleridge composed his great poem 'Kubla Khan'. Coleridge himself related how, in 1797, 'the Author, then in ill health, had retired to a lonely farm-house between Porlock and Linton [sic], on the Exmoor confines of Somerset and Devonshire'. It was an area the poet walked many times. On this stay, probably in early October of that year, Coleridge combined his usual prodigious reading with a quantity of laudanum taken to alleviate 'a slight indisposition'. He later recollected reading 'the following sentence, or words of the same substance' from Samuel Purchas's *Pilgrimage*, an early 17th century volume of travel writing and folk myths: 'Here the Kubla Khan commanded a palace to be built, and a stately garden thereunto. And thus ten miles of fertile ground were inclosed with a wall'. Then the poet succumbed to three hours of sleep. Sleep – he added – 'at least of the external senses'. He later believed that during this reverie he had composed two to three hundred lines of verse. On waking, Coleridge 'instantly and eagerly' wrote down the lines that many of us read, and even learned by heart, at school.

They begin, of course:
In Xanadu did Kubla Khan
A stately pleasure dome decree:
Where Alph, the sacred river, ran
Through caverns measureless to man
   Down to a sunless sea…

As we also learned at school, the writing was brought to an end by the visit of 'a person on business from Porlock'. When the latter departed after an hour, Coleridge found with dismay that he could no longer recall the verses yet to be written down. The 'person from Porlock' has become a universal excuse for literary non-performance. It was irresistible: my wife and I decided to make a pilgrimage to Ash Farm.

Arriving on an early April afternoon in the protracted 'Spring' of 2013, we were welcomed by Tony and Jenny Richards. They have run the farm since 1966 and, luckily for literary pilgrims, Jenny does B&B. They spoke amusingly about the number of visitors, often American or Japanese, who drive down to the farm from the A39 and rather unconvincingly inquire about B&B. They've got used to asking, 'Are you by any chance interested in Coleridge'. That's usually why folk have persevered with the two mile lane from the main road. (As I did myself last autumn – just to see the place. I realised I had to come back and stay.) Tony had been busy with lambing for the past few weeks – his fields were full of healthy looking lambs. The night before our arrival, he had risen at two a.m. to check on his ewes and got back to bed at four. Nonetheless, he kindly sat down with us to talk about Coleridge. He was quick to point out that Ash Farm is not necessarily the place mentioned by the poet. 'It's all conjecture,' he declared. He's right, of course. Claims have been made for other farms above Culbone, like Silcombe and Broomstreet. However, in a manuscript in the British Museum, Coleridge – a great walker – was very specific about the distance of the farm-house from Culbone Church: a quarter of a mile. This fits Ash Farm precisely, but not its rivals. Silcombe is half a mile from the church and Broomstreet some two miles distant. We had looked up the standard work by Richard Holmes, *Coleridge: Early Visions* (1989), and found that he favours Ash Farm.

Tony told us that his ancestors have farmed hereabouts for generations. The families of the Richards and the Reds are intertwined. Tony believes that R.D. Blackmore featured characters surnamed Ridd, a generic variant of Red, in *Lorna Doone* because the name was so often met with on Exmoor that no one could have complained about being the model for one of his characters. The farm had originally been known, Tony said, as Esshe – which is the name of an old Devon family but also linked etymologically to Ash. These trees are plentiful here. He recommended that we visit a fine specimen on the path down the valley to the church. He reckons it is over 200 years old. Over the years

he's seen the gate hinges, once attached, swallowed up inside the trunk as it grew over them. Tony offered to look out a book and some articles for us to see later and we set off to explore.

No sooner had we walked out of the house to photograph it than the rain began, to be followed by hail, which settled. (Tony said that this was the worst spring he could remember.) During the afternoon, we were alternately soaked then bathed in sunlight and eventually regaled with entrancing cloud formations. We took the footpath that leads from the farmyard to Culbone Combe and thence to the church. Coleridge is likely to have known this path well. He would have passed the spot where the massive Ash tree now stands. Perhaps it was an unconsidered sapling in his day.

'Kubla Khan' is among the most studied poems in any language and many books describe its legion of possible sources. The passage about Kubla Khan in Purchas contains vivid details concerning fertility rites involving the milk of white mares. However, Richard Holmes, like his namesake Sherlock, detected another major ingredient of the poem. 'Any footwalker,' Holmes wrote in his 1989 book, 'can discover the most striking topographical "source" for themselves: it lies in what might be called the erotic, magical geography of Culbone Combe seen from Ash Farm. Between the smooth curved flanks of the coastal hills, a thickly wooded gulley runs down to the sea (the "romantic chasm"), enclosing a hidden stream which gushes beneath the tiny medieval chapel of Culbone, a plague-church and "sacred site" since Anglo-Saxon and possibly pre-Christian times.' Readers of Hazel Eardley-Wilmot's *Yesterday's Exmoor* (1990) will recall the Anglo-Saxon 'wheel cross' which still stands about a mile south of Culbone Church (and is part of a prehistoric stone row).

The topography described by Holmes is pertinent to the poem's second section, charged with sexual symbolism, concerning 'that deep romantic chasm':
And from this chasm, with ceaseless turmoil seething,
As if this earth in fast thick pants were breathing,
A mighty fountain momently was forced:
Amid whose swift half-intermitted burst
Huge fragments vaulted like rebounding hail,
Or chaffy grain beneath the thresher's flail:
And 'mid these dancing ricks at once and ever
It flung up momently the sacred river.

There is a remarkable late essay on Coleridge by Ted Hughes. 'The Snake in the Oak' appears in Hughes's book of essays, *Winter Pollen* (1994). Hughes recognized the importance to Coleridge of 'the high downs over the deep romantic chasms of the Samuel Palmerish, magical, North Somerset Paradise...' Hughes explored the deep psychological roots of Coleridge's three great visionary poems – 'Kubla Khan', 'The Rime of the Ancient Mariner' and 'Christabel'. Hughes proposed that 'each poem revolves around the otherworld female'. This 'semi-supernatural figure modulates from the love-sick bringer of ecstatic joys' Hughes sees in 'Kubla Khan'. She is 'the spirit of the poet's own *incantatory language'* – his deepest creative source, which Hughes saw as opposed to the Christian values of Coleridge's 'Intellectual Self'. This was a battle between the pagan Mother Goddess and the Christian God. Hughes also saw the topography of the poem, with its caverns, sacred river and fountains, as a symbolic diagram of Coleridge's own psyche.

Reading the perceptive texts by Holmes and Hughes made me look at Ash Farm in a new light. Much has been written – and no doubt will continue to be – about which farm-house is the one at which Coleridge stayed when he wrote 'Kubla Khan'. However, the important thing is not so much the precise building but the wider location of Culbone Hill, Culbone Combe and Culbone Church. This landscape, at once pagan, Christian, erotic and spiritual was the place to which Coleridge retreated to recover from an illness and to write. It contained in dramatic external form all the forces with which he was negotiating on an inner psychological and creative level. Even though his masterpiece emerged spontaneously from the subconscious – to his great surprise and our lasting fascination – Coleridge had to be in this particular landscape to mend and create. I returned from my visit asking this: could 'Kubla Khan' have been written anywhere else than above Culbone Combe?

With warm thanks to Mr and Mrs Richards of Ash Farm, Culbone, and to Elizabeth McLaughlin for her writings on Literary Exmoor.

Ash Farm sheep.

Mark Haworth-Booth is an Honorary Research Fellow at the Victoria and Albert Museum, where he served as Curator from 1970-2004. He and his wife moved to North Devon in 2009.

FROM THE MOOR TO WORLD CHAMPION – EXMOOR PONY STALLION 'BEAR'

Dawn Westcott

In 2004, I chose a wild Exmoor pony colt foal to socialise and tame from the Moorland Mousie Trust. Who could have possibly known that this unwanted, fluffy little chap would go on to win two world championships in Horse Agility, become a prolific multi champion in the show ring, a successful sire and a wonderful riding pony? This is the story of 'Bear'.

When I first saw Hawkwell Versuvius 'Bear' (bred by Mr J. Western – Hawkwell Herd 12), he had just arrived at the Moorland Mousie Trust with other unwanted foals. They were understandably wary of their new environment and wondering what the future would hold. No longer with their familiar herd and also recently inspected and hot branded, they were not feeling particularly well disposed towards humans. I was immediately drawn to Bear who stared at me intently and my heart went out to him.

As is the way with Exmoors, Bear had chosen me and I promised him then that whatever he grew into, I'd always look after him. To cut a long story short, I saw more of him through binoculars for close to a year than I did close up, which meant he couldn't be gelded. Finally, after much patience, Bear accepted a head collar and we realised he looked like rather a good pony. He was, however, very suspicious of humans and Monty Roberts techniques such as 'advance and retreat' helped to build trust between us. But there were still many times when we 'ate mud'! On one of his first walks out he galloped off onto a large area of common. I waited and after a few minutes he came cantering back and stood there with the lunge line trailing, looking at me. I stepped forwards and picked up the line and he didn't move. I knew then that he was willing to give me a chance.

The following May (2006) I took him to the Exmoor Pony Society Stallion Parade. This was fairly hair-raising but the judges liked him enough to give him a stallion licence there and then. Soon afterwards, he stood Champion Exmoor at Devon County Show and later that year stood Overall Supreme Champion at the Exmoor Pony Society Breed Show. Since then, he has won numerous championships at county and national level, including another Supreme In Hand Breed Show win in 2010. In 2011, he stood Overall Reserve Supreme Champion and Gold medal winner in the National Pony Society Kilmannan Stud Mountain & Moorland In Hand Silver Medal Championship Final.

Bear lives naturally with mares and foals all year round and has produced some lovely progeny, including two licensed stallion sons, Cheritonridge Mont de Brouilly and Anchor Fee Fi Fo Fum.

Starting Bear to saddle was somewhat tricky as he was reluctant to accept a rider. He accepted the tack, but as soon as anything approaching a rider appeared, he was off. We decided to make a dummy rider, so Boris was constructed, but even after a careful introduction, this produced an explosive reaction and Bear dispensed with Boris, leaving him in pieces all around the arena. Bear watched quietly while we rebuilt him. Soon 'Mark from the Household Cavalry' was ready to ride and this time Bear accepted the dummy rider. This was a real turning point and soon after that, we had a rider on and were away.

We believe that Bear's fear-based responses are rooted in his experience of being multiple hot branded as a foal. Exmoors have to endure a number of branded marks applied with red hot irons and no pain relief, which can leave them with an inherent fear of the memory of lasting pain. Things are slowly changing but the campaign continues to reduce branding to a single pony/herd ID management mark, and to cease the hot branding of domestically born Exmoors. Interestingly, when we started his unbranded stallion son Monty to saddle, he displayed none of these fear-based behaviours. Progressing Bear's ridden work has taken time and patience and we've learned that there are no shortcuts in producing a moorbred Exmoor pony stallion who is forward-thinking and enthusiastic in his work.

Horse Agility groundwork has proved important in developing trust and confidence with Bear. This involves a horse and handler navigating a course of challenging obstacles, in a head collar and rope with the ultimate aim being to work 'at liberty' in open countryside and wilderness areas. In 2011 we entered an International Horse Agility League competition and, each month, filmed set courses and competed against horses and ponies from across the world. In 2011 and 2012, Bear and I won the world championship. The resulting bond and understanding achieved has enabled Bear to flourish and also means he can ride out and take part in equestrian activities in a bitless bridle which we use wherever rules allow us. We are now concentrating on Bear's ridden work and are looking forward to seeing what he can achieve in the ridden show ring.

With their exceptional intelligence and independent characters, Exmoor ponies show a real aptitude for equestrian performance activities, particularly when trained with positive, trust-based methods. Living wild on the moors, they have to navigate natural obstacles, solve problems and work things out for themselves – the perfect training ground! Bear has demonstrated clearly that it pays dividends to be respectful and understanding of the way we treat Exmoor ponies – ideally from the moment we bring them off the moors and in their subsequent handling and training. Exmoor ponies are the closest relative to the North West European Prehistoric horse and they remain on the

endangered breeds list, so we should treasure the opportunity to interact with these amazing creatures.

To find out more about Hawkwell Versuvius and Holtball Exmoor Pony Stud, visit www.exmoorponyclub.co.uk

Nick & Dawn Westcott own Holtball Exmoor Pony Stud (Herd 11) and farm in the Porlock Vale. Dawn is the founder of Equinetourism.co.uk, Equines At Liberty and the Exmoor Pony Club, double International Horse Agility Club World Champion (2011 and 2012) with moor bred Exmoor Pony stallion, Hawkwell Versuvius, and an equine trainer qualified in Monty Roberts horsemanship techniques.

THE LUCY PERRY AWARDS

Christopher Whinney

Each year the Exmoor Society offers cash prizes to children in the Exmoor area to write about Exmoor. Thanks to the generosity of our sponsor, the family of Lucy Perry, we are in a position to give awards of £60 for first, £40 for second and £25 for third, to children aged 9 to 11 and also to children aged 12 to 14. We contact 26 schools in and around Exmoor encouraging them to get their children to write either in poetry or prose, something original about Exmoor, its wild life, fauna and flora, or its landscape or its characteristics.

Last year we had 112 entries from five schools: Great Torrington, Dulverton Middle School, North Molton Primary School, West Buckland, Kingsmead School Wiveliscombe, and one independent entry.

We are aware that time is limited in the School Curriculum especially for extra things, and that teachers are very busy people, and so we are most grateful to them for their help in promoting this award. The Executive puts environmental education very high on their priorities, and feel that time spent getting children to think about Exmoor is time well spent. Some of these children will grow up to be the farmers and caretakers of Exmoor.

Many are the references to the Exmoor Beast – too many as far as the judges are concerned, but close behind is the Exmoor Emperor –
   The Emperor of Exmoor proud and brave
   Did the hunter chase you to your grave?

The deer and ponies get many observations, but also the rivers of Exmoor and 'the salmon swimming against the rushing waters'.

One entry which dealt with the 'senses' of Exmoor caught the judges' eye –
   I can feel Exmoor
   Like red velvet
   Rubbing against my skin.

While another commented on the 'sounds' of Exmoor and mentioned the 'shouting, the shooting, the beating, the yaw of the stag, the grunt of the pig, the groan of the cow', contrasting with the 'tractors are rumbling and the Landrovers are rattling and the pubs are full of people chatting'.

There is much about the atmosphere of Exmoor, 'the looming, misty moor' but two entries were extolling the virtues of Dartmoor. However the judges felt that these children at least are well acquainted with the wonders of Exmoor and more than able to express their feelings in words.

UP ON EXMOOR WITH MY DOG

Emily Coles, Kingsmead School, Wiveliscombe

You could say walking a dog is a chore,
Sometimes it's a bit of a bore,
Dog on lead, tugging you along,
Morning and night, when the birds sing their song,
Walking up on Exmoor each day,
In all months, August, January and May.

Every time not taking a look around,
Not taking in the sight and sound,
Rushing to get home for a cup of tea,
Well... you're missing out on the beauty we can see,
It's an amazing place on our doorstep,
Not just a place we can walk our pet.

That's why I love when family come to stay,
All the way from London every May,
I love it when I take the dog for a walk on the hill,
They think it's stunning and the walk is a thrill,
They take pictures of the average pheasant and bunny,
They love the taste of the fresh, local honey.

They come every morning and night,
Just to take a glimpse of this stunning sight,
The trees, the flowers, the animals and streams,
It's not just a chore as it seems,
So next time you're out walking your dog on Exmoor,
Take a peep at the beauty so it's a treat not a chore.

Think of them in London walking their dog up the street,
They don't see wonders at their feet,
How lucky we are to live so near,
How every morning I want to be here,
Hiding behind trees looking at deer,
That's where I want to be, just...here.

You could say dog walking is a chore,
Sometimes it's a bit of a bore,
Dogs on lead, tugging you along,
Morning and night, when the birds sing their song,
Walking on Exmoor each day,
In all months, August, January and May.

I KNOW A PLACE
Ruby Winzer, Dulverton Middle School

I know a place
Where blackberries bloom
The sun shines in
Bursting the gloom

A brook runs shallow but strong
The hollowed oak, mighty
But sadly defeated by winter
Maple saplings bend elegantly in the whistling wind

In the heart of Exmoor
The trees carve a glen
This is the place
Where blackberries bloom!

ENPA REPORT

Nigel Stone

Over the past year, the National Park Authority has successfully implemented a major restructuring of the staff team and we now employ around 60 full time equivalent (FTE) staff, compared to 80 FTE two years ago.

The staff have continued to show their commitment to Exmoor and have worked well during an unsettling period. When considering our structural changes we were keen to ensure that we have the capacity to continue to deliver services to a high standard and to build on our close links with the local community, particularly the farming community who have such a key role in caring for the National Park environment.

Farming is never easy and the past year has been no exception. The poor summer of 2012 followed by the December floods, January snow and very cold March made life especially difficult for sheep farmers. Poor lamb prices in the autumn were followed by a difficult lambing season in early spring when the cold weather meant that there was little fresh grass at a critical time in the farming year.

The next twelve months is likely to be a crucial time for farming as the review of the Common Agricultural Policy (CAP) comes towards its conclusion. The review will shape the form of farm payments and agri-environment schemes for the next 10 years and it is vital for most Exmoor farmers that the upland areas of England are better supported than has been the case over the past ten years. Over the coming months, the National Park Authority will be doing what it can to help influence government policy to benefit farmers on Exmoor.

2012 also saw the adoption of a new Partnership Plan for Exmoor 2012-17. The Plan is the result of close involvement from a large number of partner organisations and sets out the 12 agreed priorities for Exmoor for the next five years under the banner – **"Working Together for Exmoor"**.

The Authority's role will be primarily one of supporting local communities and other organisations in their work to benefit Exmoor. One way we do this is by providing funding support and, over the past 12 months, just over £400,000 has been provided by the National Park Authority for local projects. Examples include:

- £30,000 to Quantock Motors for the **Exmoor Coastal Link 300 Bus Service** with the aim of providing a long-term economically viable service without the need for further public funding.

- **Landscape Conservation Grants** to around 50 local farmers and landowners for hedge management and other conservation projects.

- Just over £16,000 to Dulverton & District Civic Society for a permanent **Red Deer Exhibition** at the Heritage Centre in Dulverton – the first such exhibition for Exmoor's truly 'iconic' symbol.

- £50,000 of matching funding to secure a further £250,000 from the Heritage Lottery Fund for a heritage interpretation project based at the new **Lynmouth Pavilion**.

At the time of writing (April 2013), rebuilding of the new National Park Centre at Lynmouth was making good progress and aiming for an opening during August 2013 for the peak tourism period. Our aim is that the centre should be open all year round and we hope that the planned displays, exhibitions and events will mean that the Pavilion becomes an important attraction for local people and visitors to the National Park.

Another key focus for the National Park Authority over the next few years will be on Simonsbath. During April 2013, West Somerset Council agreed to sell the former school site in Simonsbath to the National Park Authority as it became clear that it would not be possible to put together a viable housing scheme for the site at the same time as conserving its historic interest.

The National Park Authority will be undertaking conservation works to the building over the next 18 months to 2 years while plans are worked out for the area in future. We are currently working with the Parish Council and local community to work up ideas for the future of the site.

The former school site has its origins as a 'rustic dwelling' and 'grotto' in the landscaped gardens of the Simonsbath estate being developed by the Knight family in the early 1800s. We hope that we can restore the buildings and provide public access so that, when combined with the many other locations of interest such as the sawmill and pound building, Simonsbath can become an even more interesting destination in the centre of the National Park.

We intend that the project should be led and managed by a local group and would be pleased to hear from anyone who would like to play a part in the development of the project.

Nigel Stone: Chief Executive at Exmoor National Park Authority since 1999, he holds a PhD in Zoology. Before coming to the ENPA he acted as joint Chief Executive at North Dorset.

BOOK REVIEWS

THE QUANTOCKS

by Peter Haggett
240 pages,109 text figures + 16 colour plates (236 images in all)
Published by the author at The Point Walter Press,
5 Tun Bridge Close, Chew Magna, NE Somerset, England
BS40 8SU
Tel: 01275 332780 pointwalterpress@gmail.com
ISBN: 978-0-9573352-0-2

So aptly claimed to be 'a biography of a place' this fascinating
book is a veritable encyclopaedia that highlights all aspects of
the diverse country on and around the Quantock Hills. Peter
Haggett has known this region intimately for a lifetime.
Indeed, included among the copious illustrations there is a
splendid 1949 picture of the author and hiking chums wearing school ties and tweed
jackets. Now, after an academic career Professor Haggett, a geographer, reveals his
'Eight Desert Island Choices' of walks, buildings to visit and relevant best books.

All aspects of this regional study are attractively presented. It's a pleasure to read about
the history of the area, follow the physical shaping of the landscape and ponder
proposed developments for nuclear power here. One could spend hours enjoying the
photographs and planning excursions.

Who knows, perhaps one day, this book will inspire a comparable, definitive study of
Exmoor...

Peter R. Pay

FERN FEVER: THE STORY OF PTERIDOMANIA

by Sarah Whittingham
256 pages, 287mm x 230mm, 150 illustrations in colour and b/w
Hardback, published by Frances Lincoln 2012
ISBN: 9780711230705

Why do we have the Exmoor Society, the Exmoor National
Park and Exmoor as we know it? The answer could be 'Ferns'.
I have a little book by Charlotte Chanter called 'Ferny
Combes', written in 1858 'for the votaries of health and pleasure, not for votaries of Science'. It is designed 'to lead the
youthful and to cheer the weary spirit, by leading them, with
a woman's hand, to the Ferny Combes and Dells of Devon,

where my (the author's) best reward will be their innocent amusement or their restoration to health under the soothing influences of a rambling Tour'. Not exactly Clare Balding's language, but it is the fore-runner of what we still come across all over Exmoor today - interpretive literature, rambles with an educational purpose, talks on flora and fauna...

Charlotte Chanter, wife of the Rector of Ilfracombe, was the sister of Charles Kingsley. He came up with the term *Pteridomania*, fern fever, in 1855. Sarah Whittingham explains the story: her introduction shows how ferns ticked all the boxes for a mania which covered much of the Victorian and Edwardian era. Its origins can be seen in the picturesque aesthetic, the love of Nature (Wordsworth's poems mentioned varieties), the smaller gardens of the middle classes, technological developments (closely-glazed Wardian cases and stove houses for nurserymen led by Loddiges Nursery - yes, in Hackney), and the resulting successful import of ferns from all over the Empire and the world. There were three key elements in the intellectual popularisation: books which commanded large sales, particularly by George Francis and Edward Newman, cheap transportable microscopes, and railways which provided access to ferny combes by individual holidaymakers and huge numbers in Field Clubs. Upholding the craze was 'natural theology' which gave Pteridomania a highly moral respectability. 'It was constantly asserted that there was no better group of plants to study than ferns in order to achieve a closer knowledge of God'. By indulging in this activity of rational recreation the participants were showing good taste, refinement, elegance and delicacy with God's approval: wow!

After the breathless romp of an Introduction the book is divided into three sections: Collecting, Cultivating and Ferns for All. The last section is about ferns in the public sphere – did you know that the mottled raised pattern on Huntley and Palmers' custard creams was inspired by ferns? Look at these illustrations and you'll never see the world quite the same again. The section on the Cultivation of Ferns deals with all aspects from the small domestic display case to the massive municipal and private glasshouses.

I was hoping for more in the section on Collecting. People collected ferns to plant in their fernery, (or had ferns collected for them, and you can imagine where that led), or to press in an album. There are about fifty species of fern native to Britain, but it is the nature of ferns to produce 'sports', so there was a huge number of varieties for enthusiastic collectors to pursue. The author talks about the fern collectors' exploits, and reviews the main areas of collecting (only three pages on Devon around Lynmouth), but there are many questions begged.

As with seaweeding it was possible for young ladies to indulge in fern collecting unchaperoned; there's a lovely illustration of a young lady and man collecting in a verdant bower in Australia, and their eyes are on each other rather than the fern that they have collected. It is such a contrast to the picture of the all-male meeting of the British Pteridological Society; no women, why? And there is little mention of Field Clubs and their impact. The story is told in Chester, near my childhood home, of how Charles Kingsley, then Canon of Chester and wildly popular President of its Field Club, made a ruling that all train travel on its outings should be second class, overcoming the tradition that clergy travelled first class and thereby bringing town and cathedral into a happier relationship.

The author mentions the depredations of the fern collectors (one from Kent came and removed 5cwt from Devon!), and the byelaws made by Devon County Council in 1905-6 under its Chairman, Lord Fortescue, but she doesn't assess the longer-term impact. It is acknowledged that slow-growing alpine Woodsias from the north, and Killarney ferns in Ireland have never recovered, but I don't know about more local examples.

There are fascinating things in this book, but its weakness is that it presents fern fever as a bubble which burst in the early years of the twentieth century. The recently urbanised Victorians wanted access to the countryside, they were willing to learn, they liked a moral underpinning of what they were doing, they started to take legislative measures to protect species. All these things have continuities and resonances with what goes on today, and the pursuit of these threads would have been interesting.

If you have been a victim of fern fever you will want this lavishly illustrated large format book. But for most Exmoor lovers it provides little information on the area, and Sarah Whittingham's book in the Shire Library series is an attractive alternative introduction to the subject with much of the same material – modestly priced and not demanding an outsize book shelf.

Michael Gee

A SINGULAR EXMOOR MAN - HECTOR HEYWOOD
by Bruce Heywood
160 pages, 297x210mm, with many illustrations
Hardback, published by Ryelands, 2012
ISBN 978 1 906551 32 2

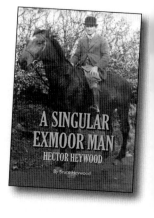

Writing a biography can never be easy, because nobody ever truly knows another person, especially those in their own family. And, in the case of this book, the author Bruce Heywood is writing about his father Hector, who - you increasingly realise as you make your way through the book - was, indeed, a singular and often extremely difficult man. Furthermore, the author was hampered by not having much written information to hand from the years before his own birth, although he was fortunate that quite a number of people were still alive who remembered Hector.

Bruce was inspired to write the book by his son Oliver who, in 2007, asked for a photograph of his grandfather and 'a few notes about him'. It starts by tracing back Hector's forebears to John Heywood – in Hector's words 'a bugger for the whisky' – who, in the mid-1800s, was farming at Lower Kemps, Winsford. John and his wife Mary had ten children, the fifth of whom was Hector's father Sidney, who married Elizabeth Bawden, and whose sister Elizabeth married Mary's brother Ernest Bawden, the famous huntsman of the Devon & Somerset Staghounds.

Sidney and Mary farmed at Hinham (now Hinam) near Dulverton and had six children, the second of whom was Frederick in 1903 and the third Hector in 1905. In 1912 the tragedy occurred that was to affect Hector for the rest of his life. He and Frederick were larking about when Frederick fell and cut himself very badly. Despite everything the doctor and hospital could do, he died two weeks later of a concealed haemorrhage. Hector blamed himself and Bruce writes: 'Hector was a troubled soul ever since then and showed remarkably selfish behaviour, even narcissistic as has been suggested by the psychotherapist Tim Williams.'

Hector helped on the farm from an early age, becoming skilled in sheep shearing, hedge laying, ploughing, snaring and shooting rabbits, tracking and hunting deer. He learned to drive and bought himself a model T Ford, following the hunt by car, the first car-follower, according to his cousin Percy Bawden. After his mother's death in 1933 he took up bird-nesting and egg-collecting, an interest that continued throughout his life and involved incredibly daring feats of tree and cliff climbing to reach the most out-of-the-way nests. He could identify the sex and age of a deer just from its slots and track an animal even across a tarmac road. In 1935 he started to take an active part in harbouring for the D&S Staghounds and was appointed official Harbourer in 1938, often riding over 60 miles a day.

It was presumably through the hunt that he met Joan Nicholson, who came from a wealthy brewing family. 'As chalk is to cheese, so Joan and her background was to Hector and his background', Bruce writes. Despite this, they married in 1940 and moved into Cloutsham. Nothing in Joan's life had prepared her for the hardship of those wartime years on a primitive farm, with a husband who did nothing at all to help in the home, showing more affection for his dogs than any human being.

Joan stuck it out for five years, during which time Bruce and his sister Beth were born, then in 1945 she gave Hector the ultimatum – either he must quit the hunt or the farm. He quit the farm and she took the children and went to stay with relatives. Eventually she relented and came back to Hector and they moved to West Luccombe.

In 1947 he stopped harbouring and became a self-employed farm labourer. Increasingly he lived, as Bruce describes it, 'by the law of Hector'. He still did nothing to help Joan, practically or financially, but he was not unkind to his children, especially when they were young. He suffered increasingly from depression and several times tried to commit suicide. In 1978 Joan died and Hector's health went downhill. He died in 1988.

Throughout the book I had the feeling that I was finding out the facts about Hector at the same time as Bruce. I found myself forming my own opinion of him as I went along, all the time thinking, 'I should not pass judgment on someone I have never met.' I am glad that Bruce sums up his own conclusions in the final chapter and hope that he not only learned a lot along the way but found the personal journey cathartic.

This book is well written, thoughtfully structured and deserves to become a classic. Much more than 'just' a biography, it tells the history of hill farming and stag-hunting over a couple of centuries, as well as painting full and vivid sketches of numerous well-known and lesser-known Exmoor characters. It does not assume knowledge on the part of the outsider, nor talk down to those readers who are Exmoor born and bred. I hope it will inspire others to write their family histories for future generations, even if their ancestors were rather less colourful.

Jenny Gibson

FOR EVER IN GREEN PASTURES
by Christopher Tull
190 pages, £8.99
Paperback, published by Broad Street Publishing, 2012
ISBN 978-0-9557019-8-6

This fourth and final novel in the Jack Longfield series continues in the same enjoyable, light-hearted but thought-provoking style as its predecessors, and moves the story of this Devonshire country vicar forward into the 1980s. Although you will have missed a treat if you have not read the previous three, *For Ever in Green Pastures* can be read on its own.

Christopher Tull is the son of a country rector and was himself ordained just over fifty years ago, spending all his ministry in rural Devon. Now retired, he lives in Challacombe and remains active in church life. He is swift to point out that the characters in his novels are all fictitious (especially the unforgettable Uncle Tiddly!) but does admit that the inspiration for them came from people he has been privileged to meet during the course of his life. It is certainly obvious from the book that he must have had many lively discussions and encounters during his career.

A couple of things in particular struck me during my reading of Jack Longfield books. One was it is nothing new for rectors/vicars to have several parishes to look after. Another was that, during the period covered by the books, the church was very much more at the heart of the rural community than it appears to be now. And, thirdly, what a very good rector Mr Tull must have been if these are the memories he has brought with him into his retirement.

Five of the Jack Longfield stories have recently been recorded for BBC Radio Devon, narrated by John Nettles. They would make a lovely "Talking Book".

Tony Gibson

VILLAGE SCHOOLING IN SOMERSET: *Learn 'em Hard*
by Sarah Villiers
224 pages, £24.99
Hardback, published by Ryelands
ISBN978-1-906551-33-9

The story of how schooling developed is fundamental to life today. It seems inconceivable that education has not always been highly valued and available to all, yet the journey to reach the point at which we are now has been arduous and long. Sarah Villiers undertook a project about that journey which will be of interest to many: to produce a book about the history of village schools in Somerset. It took three years of painstaking research during which she trawled the records at Somerset Record Office, travelled the county extensively and interviewed people.

Having amassed the information the author had to consider how to present it in two hundred pages. Sarah Villiers' decision was to divide the county into nine geographical areas and select at least one school for which she had found adequate records from each area. Thus there is a good representation of the historic county of Somerset. Of particular interest to *Exmoor Review* readers will be Skilgate and Cutcombe.

The book is divided into five parts: The Framework of Development of Schooling in Somerset; Philanthropists and Pioneers; Changing Patterns of C19th Schooling; and Forwards or Backwards – Recent Years. These comprise ten chapters. A prologue subtitled "aims and sources" precedes them while an epilogue, appendices, references and index of key people and villages follow.

The development of village schools was at its height in the 19th century when village populations were growing and the size of families increasing. There was growing concern that all should have access to a good basic education. Funding for this and support from local influential people was the key to the success and progress made in any village or group of villages. Thereafter followed formalised training for staff, and guidelines for the curriculum. These foundations paved the way for education as it is today.

Many difficulties were encountered, with one Head reporting that the children shivered and cried from the cold in 1912, another that the room was so dark that writing lessons had to be abandoned in 1910. The nurse, doctor and school inspectors were regular and unpopular visitors. There were, however, the successes and the treats, sports, concerts and visits from visitors who came to help and encourage.

It is an informative and interesting read, a sound historical work, and presented clearly, in a way that makes it a pleasure to read.

Bob and Jacqueline Patten

SIR JOHN AMORY'S STAGHOUNDS
by Richard Lethbridge MBE
160 pages, £24.99
Hardback, published by Ryelands
ISBN 978-1-906551-34-6

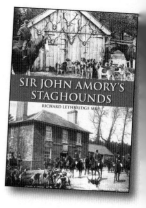

Sir John Amory's Staghounds were established in 1896 at the suggestion of the Master of the Devon and Somerset Staghounds to hunt an area of about thirty miles by twenty miles south of their country (there was no wire). This pack was unique at the time in that it was hunted entirely by amateurs, the huntsman being Sir John Amory's son Mr. Ian Heathcoat Amory and brothers Messrs Albert and Manuel de Las Casas his two whips. In 1911 Captain Harry Amory took over as huntsman when Ian was invited to take on the Mastership of the Tiverton Foxhounds and the pack continued until 1915 when Captain Harry went to war.

This was the golden age of hunting, hounds and horses were hacked many miles to and from meets with the occasional use of the railway. After one run of about thirty miles recorded in1906 from Tiverton to Honiton the field of forty or fifty faced a ride home of more than three hours. In November 1910 following a meet at Chawleigh the pack hunted for three and a half hours between Worlington, Lapford and South Molton after which it was reported that 'hounds had an eighteen miles trot back to kennels. However a good tea at Alswear started us all upon our various journeys in a happy and contented frame of mind, and with a steadfast determination to come out hunting again as soon as possible'. Riders, horses and hounds must have been phenomenally fit!

At an invitation meet near Okehampton hounds and horses left Tiverton by special train at 8am. A staghunt in that area was such a novelty that close upon a thousand people were present, some of the farmers being mounted on cart horses or Dartmoor ponies. It is recorded that 'spills were numerous. One rider had the misfortune to be immersed in the Torridge owing to the bank giving way under his horse's weight…and one horse in falling took its owner right under the water'. The day ended at Town Mills, Torrington, hounds were taken back to Beaford where Mr Amory telegraphed for a special train to meet them at South Molton Road station (Kingsnympton). Tiverton was reached at about 9pm.

Richard Lethbridge's book is beautifully presented with excellent pen and ink drawings and many fascinating photographs. He writes a very good overview of the history of Sir John Amory's Staghounds and the two hundred and fifteen records of the various runs make interesting and entertaining reading. Many of the names of people recorded will be familiar to those local to the area and with a map to hand the reader can follow the course of some truly great hunting days.

This book is a record and a celebration of a glorious period in hunting history, gone for ever, and they all seem to have had so much fun.

Anna Whinney

Meet at South Molton Station. Sir John Amory's Staghounds

A meet at the Gidley Arms Inn near Meshaw 1907. Sir John Amory's Staghounds

OBITUARIES

MICHAEL HAWKINS OBE
CHAIRMAN, EXMOOR SOCIETY 1995-2003

Michael Hawkins was born in 1927 in Minehead. His grandfather Fred established himself as a horse dealer and hunting and livery-stable proprietor at the Plume of Feathers Stables. With a family tradition of coaching, it was perhaps inevitable that Fred's sons Bill – Michael's father – and Jack, should set themselves up in the transport business when they returned from the First World War. They created the renowned Scarlet Pimpernel coach line, much loved and still fondly remembered. Michael later remarked that part of his task in his professional career involved restricting the intrusion of coaches into Exmoor and Dartmoor National Parks: "If my father and his brother ever thought my role... was even remotely disloyal to the family tradition, they were kind enough not to say so." Transport and Exmoor were thus established from the outset as twin poles in Michael's life.

Following his education at Minehead Grammar School, surprisingly Michael chose not to join his father, but instead determined on a career in public service. After serving articles at Exmouth and becoming qualified in civil and highway engineering and town planning, he eventually came to Torquay in 1957, becoming Borough Engineer and Planning Officer in 1965. Promotion came through successive waves of local government reorganisation and in due course Michael became County Engineer to the new Devon County Council and shortly afterwards County Planning Officer as well. His period at the helm coincided with the rapid expansion of motorway and major trunk routes, whilst maintaining the largest road network of any county. In 1987 his achievement was recognised when he was awarded the OBE.

In retirement Michael was able to devote more attention both to Exmoor and to rather more esoteric, transport-related projects. He became Chairman of the Exmoor Society in 1995 and was a steady hand at the tiller for some eight years. His chairmanship was firm – he came with a somewhat fearsome reputation from his Council days – yet he was, in truth, a very benign figure who, whilst standing no nonsense, was keen to seek consensus if it could possibly be achieved. In many respects he was the right man at the right time. His local government background meant that he understood entirely the pressures under which the National Park Authority and its staff laboured; equally, he could perceive readily areas in which the Authority might act differently and more effectively. The relationship between the Authority and the Exmoor Society was therefore placed in a stronger and more cooperative position. One aspect of this closer relationship was the involvement of the Society in the project to conserve and enhance the West Somerset Mineral Railway, a major part of which had been bought by the Authority in 1998.

Michael became chairman of the project planning group in 2002, and played a major role in securing an HLF grant of £46,000 to prepare the various Plans for the railway's conservation and public access.

Another labour of love was the authorship – with Roger Grimley – of *A Century of Coaching on Exmoor: "Horner Woods for Tea"*, a warm tribute to the coaching business of his family and their contemporaries. With it he united both his professional understanding of transport with his deep appreciation of Exmoor, the land of his fathers, even when in exile in Torquay never far from his heart.

Steven Pugsley

ALBERT BEER, AN EXMOOR MAN REMEMBERED

Albert Beer on the farm in 1957

The 6th July last year found me in one of my favourite places, Great Champson at Molland, for a farm walk. In 2011 my father Albert Beer and I had nominated the Dart family for the Samuel Foss Conservation Award and this was an opportunity for us to get together, to celebrate, to have fun, to learn and experience new, old and familiar things, just like the other events that he and his wife Viv ran, such as the North Devon Show. It was good to see Albert. That spring he had had a serious bout of pneumonia and had almost died. Since then he had not been feeling as full of life as he might have, but my mother Vivian and sister Susan said that he came back up the motorway a different man, somehow refreshed. He stayed that way until he died on March 15 2013 - he was 78. In the end, the heart that had powered him round Athletics tracks, across Bideford Bridge in the Bridge Race, over Exmoor in no end of cross country runs whilst at West Buckland School and over the try line for Barnstaple Rugby Football Club, just slowed down and stopped. Not that he would want us to be sad; Albert was born into a strong Christian family, a faith that sustained him.

That day at Molland had obviously been very special for Albert and what I would like to do is to explain why I think he went home smiling, as this gives an insight into who he was, and the values that underpinned what he did. Firstly the Darts' farming operation is a family concern with generations working together, passing on skills and knowledge to each other. With family and friends came hospitality and, of course, good food. When we finished the farm walk at Great Champson we returned to tables groaning under the weight of an authentic Devon tea. Albert had a love of food and understanding of the food supply-chain and the need for producers to connect to consumers. There was also a love of things local best seen at Great Champson with its Devon Cattle, Closewool and Exmoor Horn sheep, and Exmoor Ponies. For him the livestock represented a living heritage; a social, economic and genetic link back through the generations; something he understood at first hand, having worked in the industry all his life in so many roles.

Ultimately that day was about friendship. At Albert's Memorial Service the Rev. Philip Buckland quoted John 10:10, "I have come that they may have life, and have it to the full." That was what Albert was all about, helping to bring life to people in all its fullness. In 2010 Albert and Vivian celebrated their Golden Wedding and raised money to send a dairy cow to a family in Africa. In memory and celebration of Albert's life, friends and family have donated £1,500 which will pay for two dairy cows – almost a herd! Dad will be smiling. Oh happy day. Oh happy day!

Sean Beer

TIMOTHY DAVEY, OBE

Tim Davey was born in 1930 in Bristol. His family moved to Exmouth at the start of the War and then he attended Kelly College at Tavistock. He was therefore a Westcountryman, through and through.

Despite this, Tim enjoyed a far-flung career which took him to many corners of the globe. Having become a chartered surveyor, firstly in Sussex (during which period he married Wendy) and then in Pembrokeshire, he then departed for a succession of overseas postings. He began with the UN in New York where he worked with the conciliation Commission for Palestine. Then (following an interlude in the Valuation Office in Somerset) he joined the Overseas Development Administration leading to a spell of five years in Mauritius, establishing a Valuation and Rating Department and setting up a Land Valuation course in the local university. This was followed by five years in Zambia as Chief Valuation Officer and nine years in Fiji where he reorganised and managed the Land Administration system. In both countries he again established relevant university courses. Even after retiring in 1985, Tim continued to work in this field, in the Falklands, the West Indies, The Gambia and finally Bulgaria. He was awarded the OBE for his services in 1982.

Tim and Wendy retired to Withypool in 1984, having had a house there for some years. With his customary energy and public spirit, Tim immersed himself in local life – the church, singing, the parish council, serving on several local trusts and the Executive Committee of the Exmoor Society, where he offered wise counsel over many years. He and Wendy became great friends of Hope Bourne, helping her considerably in her move from Ferny Ball into Withypool village and generally keeping a watchful eye over her affairs. Tim was one of the executors of Hope's will, and helped to ensure the smooth transfer of her estate to the Exmoor Society as she had wished.

Tim was a great countryman, fascinated by wildlife and a passionate ornithologist. He was a physically big man, and sometimes this – coupled with the strength of his views – could make him seem a trifle intimidating. Yet he was possessed of the kindest and most generous heart, dedicated to the well-being of others. Without being strident, he made a significant and quietly long-lasting impact on the life of his home community and the wider Exmoor environment, and he will be much missed.

Steven Pugsley

LADY MARGARET FORTESCUE

The death of Lady Margaret Fortescue on the 27th May 2013 has finally brought to a close the family name and the synonymous link it had with Exmoor. It was of course in 1886 that Lady Margaret's grandfather, the 4th Earl Fortescue, purchased the Exmoor Forest Estate from Fredric Knight who along with his father had reclaimed a considerable tranche of this land, evidence of which remains to this day. The Fortescue family sold the last of their land holding in 1995 but the memories, the people, the influence over all these years were a treasure held dear by Lady Margaret.

Her first experiences of Exmoor were as a young girl, when the family had to move to Simonsbath House in 1934, following a tragic fire at Castle Hill. This was a cherished time of dogs, ponies, of family and friends gathering to enjoy all that Exmoor could offer. It was much later, in fact in 1958, that the responsibility of land ownership fell to her through the untimely death of her parents and one which she exercised with considerable success. The landholding was reduced to 10,000 acres as a result of death duties and Simonsbath became the centre of the in-hand farming activity. It was a time of expansion in agriculture and Lady Margaret was keen to exploit all the avenues available to make this large hill farm a successful business and one in which all those involved with it over the years had a great sense of pride. Monthly meetings were held in the Estate office at Castle Hill but visits to Simonsbath to see what was going on, on the ground, held much more interest for her and when the weather was favourable she would ride out over the forest with Sante Lafuente and get a better perspective of the reality of things.

Lady Margaret's love of Exmoor was not confined to her own farming interests, she was a founder member of the Exmoor Society, evidence of which can be found in the first edition of the Review in 1959 when her membership cost one guinea! A great supporter of the two forest packs of hounds, she was president of the Exford Show and every year could be found there, presenting the prizes and in particular the Fortescue Perpetual Challenge Cup for the Champion horse in show. As a patron of St Luke's, Simonsbath, she would rarely miss sharing in the harvest festival and carol services. The esteem in which she was held was in evidence when several hundred gathered at Filleigh on the 7th June 2013 for a service of Thanksgiving for her life and service to the community. The finality of this era resounded in the huntsman's blowing of 'Gone Away'.

Ron Smith

TOM ROOK

Thomas William Rook was born in Porlock in 1928, the son of Herbert Rook, landlord of the Ship Inn, which his grandfather had run. His mother, a Partridge, was one of a farming family of 13 from Romansleigh who moved to Selworthy Farm and then to Horner Farm.

Tom's father, Herbert, had a keen interest in all field sports and was held in great respect throughout Exmoor. Tom started school in Porlock and remembered his father taking him off at lunchtime to see the hounds, should they have been in the vicinity. But when Tom was only 7, his father died, leaving Tom's mother to run the pub on her own, as well as bringing up Tom and his older sister Joan.

When Tom was 10 he moved to Minehead Secondary School. The War years meant locals attended school only in the mornings, as it was used by evacuees in the afternoons, which left some afternoons free for Tom to develop his early passion for staghunting.

On leaving school Tom joined James Phillips & Sons of Town Mills Minehead, auctioneers, estate agents, corn and feed merchants, earning 10 shillings a week. He successfully completed his Estate Agent's exams by correspondence course in 1955 – no mean feat, bearing in mind his modest educational background.

In 1960 Tom married Margaret whose father was lost when his ship was sunk in the Bristol Channel. Her mother had lived in Southampton but at a young age, Margaret moved to Exmoor to live with an uncle and aunt. Tom and Margaret were soon to produce Lesley and Phillip, and Margaret combined her love of horses and dogs with bringing up her children and being a very devoted wife.

In the same year as Tom married, he became a partner in the expanding firm, which resulted in offices in Williton, Barnstaple and Minehead, the latter run by Tom. Throughout his life Tom was an extremely busy man, serving on too many committees to name, but many were related to Porlock village life and others connected to farming and staghunting. In 1959 he became secretary of the Exmoor Horn Sheep Breeders, a post he retained until 1990. He helped to form the Exmoor Suckled Calf Rearers Association and was secretary for several years.

The mainspring of Tom's successful career was his love of Exmoor, his passion for Exmoor farming and of course staghunting. Tom had a deep understanding of the trials and tribulations of hill farming on Exmoor always helping farmers whenever he could. He cleverly combined his hours of following the hunt with visiting farmers. This could mean some very long days and as a result of the warm hospitality of some Exmoor folk, the Land Rover on many occasions had to make a very cautious descent into Porlock.

In the early '80s he was approached by the BBC to make a film – 'Twelve months in the life of an Exmoor man'. How appropriate, but perhaps with his knowledge and passion for Exmoor, the title should have been 'Twelve months in the life of "The Man of Exmoor"'? The film was first shown on Christmas Day after the Queen's Speech.

In 1987 after the Estate Agency side of the business was sold, Tom, with help from Peter Huntley and others, obtained investments from a large number of Exmoor farmers, to form the Exmoor Farmers Livestock Auctions Ltd, now serving Exmoor so well, through the markets at Blackmoor Gate and Cutcombe.

While Tom's contribution to Exmoor was immense, he was a modest man and would have felt that Exmoor had given him far more than vice-versa. Tom would simply want us to carry on enjoying Exmoor and preserving it as the very special place we all enjoy so much.

Tim Yandle

JOYCE, LADY WALEY-COHEN

Joyce was the only daughter of Lord and Lady Nathan. He was a WW1 veteran, a solicitor, Member of Parliament and a Government Minister, while she was chairman of the London County Council.

Shortly after she left school, at one of the many parties she attended in London – and she never lost her love of parties – Joyce met the unforgettably charismatic figure of

Bernard Waley-Cohen. From that moment, it is said, he wooed her until she was old enough to propose to. Whether she felt the same initially is debatable. Joyce went up to Girton College Cambridge to read English. He kept every letter she wrote to him during that time, but she apparently kept none of his. They married in 1943 and over the next seven years they had four children, Rosalind, Stephen, Robert and Joanna.

Work required London to be the main family base, and so began the regular commuting to Honeymead. Joyce was a brave woman in many ways, but no more so than in this, as anyone who remembers Bernard's driving can testify. When there was a petrol shortage, she rode pillion on his motorbike, taking not a few falls, one on Exford bridge when she was expecting Stephen. In the interests of fuel economy the engine would be turned off and Joyce must have been one of the few people to know that it is possible to coast from the top of the hill at Luckwell Bridge to Exford.

In 1960 Bernard became Lord Mayor of London. Joyce was a dazzling hostess, setting an almost impossible standard of elegance and style. So successful was that year, that the only names people can now remember of anyone who held the post of Lord Mayor are Dick Whittington and Bernard.

Joyce made huge contributions in education, health, and law in the tradition of public service into which she had been born. In education, she acted as a governor in a variety of schools; she felt passionately about women's education. She served on Hospital Boards and sat as a magistrate for 50 years.

Joyce was not brought up as a countrywoman but after her marriage she became one. She learned to ride the moor and go hunting, which she continued to do until she was nearly 80. After that, she insisted that those who had been out, came in to tea afterwards, so that she could keep up with all that was happening. From the late 1980s she lived full time on her beloved Exmoor, where she was a mainstay of the local community. She set up the Craft Tent at Exford Show, took up spinning and established Honeymead Homespun.

Highly intelligent, kind, exceptionally generous and genuinely interested in her community and other people, she loved to talk and to argue with people of all ages on equal terms, and was very funny, which is probably why she had friends of every age. She was brave and intellectually rigorous. Above all she liked to know everything that was going on and she missed very little, all of which helps to explain why she became such an important part of Exmoor for as long as many can remember.

Ann Mallalieu

EMBELLE WOOD BEACH

Molly Richards

At times of stress, Nurse May came to stay with us. Outings with Nurse May were mostly to Embelle Wood beach. This was no bucket and spade beach, like the ones I had read about in storybooks, where children built sandcastles, romped and swam. Flanked by the steep wooded slope up to the farms above, Embelle Wood Beach was an area of outstanding wildness, strewn with boulders, rocks and pebbles, an area where for some reason you looked over your shoulder from time to time.

In later years, going there alone I would experience times of unease, times of almost fear, especially at high tide, when the sound of the waves ceaselessly crashing over rocks increased the sense of one's own isolation. But before this, there was Nurse May. She took us down to the beach, where we ate a few sandwiches, lit a small fire, had a bit of a paddle and maybe a careful dip, before making the long, slow, journey home. To my shame, I seem to remember that Tom and I were the two complainers: I do not recall any of the others whining as much as we two could.

Nurse May was there for the years when we were too young to go alone. When she became too old to do the long haul to the beach, she sort of melted out of our lives and went back to Sussex. She did, though, live to be well into her nineties.

After she left, we were in the tender care of David and Tom. With Louie scrubbing on hands and knees, and so many of us children wanting to go in and out of the house, she or my mother would tell us to go out and play and not to come back until dinner time, usually with the suggestion that we go to the beach. If my father happened to be around and feeling morning-afterish, any such order might be given with the aim of keeping us out of sight and out of mind. His voice could shrivel a child at ten paces. So going to the beach seemed the least bad option, and with no Nurse May to look after us, things became a little more exciting and a little more precarious.

There were times when we came near to being cut off by the tide and the race along the jagged rocks to safety, with the grey sea seeming to reach out for us as we passed. On one occasion we lost all our footwear. Putting our shoes in a pile well away from the sea, we wandered off, finding such interesting things to do that they were completely forgotten until it was time to go home. I remember the painful walk back on the rough track. I remember too the look on my mother's face when she took in the loss, and the enormity of finding the money for five new lots of footwear.

Sometimes in the fruit season we would take our walks along the beach as far as Glenthorne. Here if we were lucky, and there was no one around, we could walk home the long way, which took us alongside the orchard. No plums or apples ever tasted better and on those occasions we did not return home starving.

I remember being on the beach with Margaret and Josie when we saw a most eerie lifting and falling of something large and white across the beach between the rocks. Because there was no wind, we knew it was not a piece of white cloth waving in the breeze. We edged warily forward and, eventually, we realised that it was a huge and, to us, completely unfamiliar, bird.

Although gannets are quite usual along the high cliffs of small, isolated islands with rocky ledges, we had never seen one on Embelle Wood beach. It allowed us to lift it and measure it, to marvel at its size and great wingspan. It was beautiful, with its large eyes outlined in fine black feathers, its long, black-tipped wings and, most of all, the faintly orange head fading into white towards the clean lines of its beak.

But this was a very sick bird, too weak to scramble through the rocks. We carried it to a level spot but, although bright of eye and quite alert, it made no attempt to escape us, nor did it seem unduly worried at being carried. Next came a long argument on what we should do. Margaret said we should leave it there and let nature take its course. Josie and I both wanted to take it home. "It's a *sea* bird," Margaret insisted, "it lives on *fish*," irritating us by the pressure she put on the words sea and fish, all the more so because we knew she was right.

After she had walked off in a huff and disappeared into the dense, low, scrubby wood-land, I took control as the oldest and told Josie that we had the choice of taking the gannet down to the water's edge or taking it home with us and putting it on the pond. "If it gets better," I said, "we could bring it back and put it in the sea." Josie was about seven at the time and I was ten. We both looked doubtfully at the bird, as big as a goose, then cast our eyes up the steep sides of the wooded cliffs.

I shall always remember that journey – and so does Josie. We struggled bravely, even making light of the 900 feet climb, until we had passed the halfway position. After that there was no turning back, no admitting to a very bad mistake. When we eventually arrived at the farm, we were totally exhausted, but not so exhausted that we were incapable of justifying our actions. No one argued or challenged us, and perhaps there was even a slight admiration in the eyes of our-father-which-art.

We put the wan, sad bird on the pond, hoping to see it at least rejoice a bit by swimming a length, but no, it floated listlessly at the water's edge, refusing all food. I feel sure that, even if we had had a live sardine, it would have refused that too. After three days and innumerable visits to the pond, we found it dead one morning before school. So ended our love affair with a beautiful gannet.

Just off this beach, during the war, an oil tanker was struck by a mine, and here was horror – so far unimagined by me – of the reality of war. From the cliff top we watched the ending of many lives, while helpless aircraft hovered overhead and the sea burned all around the stricken tanker.

Another drama occurred when two ships ran aground in the fog on Embelle Wood beach. The first we knew of it was when police and coastguard vehicles rushed down our lane. Having to pause long enough to open a gate, and asked what were they hurrying for, they told us what had happened. When Margaret heard this, she took off down the lane, into the woods and straight down the cliff, clutching and falling all the way to the beach. On arrival, she was met by Greek seamen who were unable to make themselves understood. The other ship was Irish and none of their sailors had yet got ashore. Soon the police and coast guards arrived and took over. A few months later, however, Margaret was presented with a huge and splendid box of chocolates for being the first on the scene.

Here on this beach my great-uncle John Red built a boathouse and a house that was never lived in. I never knew great-uncle John, because he died before I was born, but I learned quite a lot about him from my cousin Dick Gregory.

Apparently he was a very grey man, with a grey face, a grey moustache and grey clothes. He was also a very heavy smoker. He had always spent a lot of time on the beach, looking out for what was washed ashore. Broomstreet when my parents moved in was packed in every available space with stuff brought up from the beach, including beams and planks of wood, especially hard woods. Among his many enterprises, he built limekilns and brought lime and coal from Wales in his own boat called the Eleanor Mary, which was the name my parents chose for me, although I was always known as Molly. The limestone and coal were brought ashore in smaller boats, unloaded on Embelle Wood Beach and hauled up to the kiln.

He had been most reluctant to leave Broomstreet after my parents moved in. My mother told me that in the end the only way of getting him out was to take his bed down to Littlewood, where his sister Elizabeth had already set up home. Great-uncle John, feeling confined and useless, being pensioned off and sent to live in a small cottage, with no farm to run, must have despaired. His visits to Embelle Wood and the beach were now almost a necessity. It would seem that Lady Lovelace gave great-uncle John permission to build a house on the beach. Perhaps she had smiled to herself and put the request down to the ramblings of an old man?

At some stage he must have told his sister that he was building a new house for them, and she, old and absent-minded, might not have even heard or taken in what he had said. Indeed, such a foolish thought could surely never be taken seriously? They were both old; provisions would have had to be brought from Porlock Weir or Brendon on horseback. As for great-aunt Elizabeth, she would have had to say goodbye to any visits to or from any friend or relative. There would have been just her grey brother and his eccentric grey ways. An added reason for wanting to stay around Littlewood was that my mother had started to have babies and great-aunt Elizabeth was not going to miss seeing her great-nephews and nieces grow up.

There came a time when the building was getting so far ahead that he thought it time to advise his sister of its progress. The walls of the rooms were up and the house now only required a roof. Imagine the scene when he began proudly to announce that the cottage was almost ready to move into. Elizabeth must have looked at him as if he had gone mad. Under no circumstances would she move down. "You go!" she must have screamed at him. And perhaps she said, as I might have done: "And the sooner the better." How he must have worked at his dream and how he must have grieved at its total impossibility without the help of his sister.

I wish I had known him, for it seems odd that such a grey man turned out to be such a fascinating character. The house would have been very primitive. When we children came to investigate it, quite a few years later, some tall bits of walls were still standing. Several rooms were outlined in the ruins, including a small one, presumably intended to be the lavatory. Over the years sheep and deer wandered in and out of great-uncle John's cottage. At very high tide, it must have been flooded. His boat shed was also still there, pretty tumbledown, but useful for us in the rain or to eat our sandwiches in...

Here on this beach my cousin accidentally set the hillside burning...

Here on this beach my brother found a decomposing body...

Here, by being so often on this beach, we perhaps saved our parents' sanity...

One of my regrets is that now, with negotiable tracks washed away, I am no longer able to get there.

Molly Richards grew up on Broomstreet Farm as one of six children. This excerpt is taken from her memoir, *Growing Wild on Exmoor*, published by Ryelands, which was written, she says, 'With pleasure, pain and, in parts, black humour.'

THE SOCIETY'S YEAR IN RETROSPECT

HIGHLIGHTS OF THE YEAR

Achievements and performance:

The major achievements in the current year include the following:
- Successful launch and opening of the Hope Bourne Exhibition at the Dulverton Guildhall Heritage and Arts Centre, which has generated considerable press and public interest.
- Commissioning of a 10 minute DVD "Hope Bourne – A Celebration of Exmoor".
- Publishing a book, *Hope Bourne's Exmoor: Eloquence in Art*, in which a selection of her paintings and sketches is reproduced.
- Applying to the ENPA Partnership Fund and the Heritage Lottery Fund for financial support for a project entitled "Unlocking Exmoor's Heritage".
- Taking the lead in initiating an independent report into Exmoor's woodlands in partnership with others.
- Continuing the Pinnacle Award for young people wishing to develop a business enterprise.
- Extending the Society's Walks Programme based on themes. The Lorna Doone themed walk appeared on BBC's Countryfile programme in January.
- Maintaining the campaign for Exmoor's hill farmers by supporting the drive to find ways to implement Payment for Ecosystems Services (PES) and also by raising concerns over moorland management.
- Acting on the findings of a membership survey.

The Annual Report highlights the significant contributions and activities the Society has undertaken in order to achieve its aims and objectives. The Society acts as a watchdog and a champion for Exmoor's special qualities such as beauty, wildlife, heritage, recreation and livelihoods associated with the land.

GOVERNANCE

Following the support from last year's membership survey, the Executive has continued its core work of being a watchdog and champion for the status of Exmoor as a national park. It has spent a great deal of time in developing the bid to

Pinnacle Award winners – from left to right: Rachel Thomas, Adam and Oliver Hill and Sir Antony Acland.

the Heritage Lottery Fund and the Exmoor National Park Authority (ENPA) Partnership Fund for grants to archive all the material, some of national importance, held at Parish Rooms, so that it can be used for education and research purposes as well as by the general public. We have met with representatives of many organisations to develop this project, including Somerset Records Office and the National Archives. We are very grateful for the interest and support we have received. The Executive has decided that this is the first essential step before searching for other premises. The appeal for funds to support the move has been put on hold.

Membership categories have been simplified into individual, family, corporate and life, with increased subscriptions, which have been well supported. The charity is waiting to register with the Charity Commission as a Charitable Incorporated Organisation. The Society's giving in order to further its aims stands at £176,000 in the last ten years.

Financial review for the year ended 31 May 2013
Total incoming resources for 2013 amount to £54,086 as compared with £79,489 in 2012. A decrease in the year of £20,720 in bequests and a further £5,994 in donations accounts for this reduction, with small increases in most other income sources.

Speakers at the Spring Conference, 26 April 2013.
Left to right: *Sarah Bryan, Head of Conservation ENPA; Charles Cowap, Rural Chartered Surveyor; Nigel Hester, Project Manager, National Trust; Sir Antony Acland, President Exmoor Society; Nigel Stone CE ENPA; Chris Binnie, Water Engineer; Guy Thomas-Everard, Landowner; and Lucy Hunt, Devon & Cornwall Area Manager, Environment Agency.*

The Hope Bourne Walk, 22 August 2012, on the way from Lanacre Bridge to Ferny Ball.

Resources expended amount to £59,013, as compared with £58,381 in 2012. Overheads have been well controlled this year but additional expenditure has been made regarding the Hope Bourne Exhibition which began 22 March 2013, and is ongoing and the commissioning of a DVD commemorating the work of Hope Bourne. Also, despite the decrease in income, the level of grants given, donations made and prizes awarded has been increased.

Overall, the net outgoing resources for the year amounted to £4,927 as compared with net incomings of £21,108 in the previous year.

On the balance sheet there has been an overall increase of £17,496 in total funds. An increase of £22,423 in the value of investments is responsible for this gain.

The return on the COIF investments in the year has increased on the dividend side as additional funds have been invested. The interest from deposit accounts has remained stable.

Finally, the Trustees are able to confirm that the investments are held in accordance with their powers and that at the year-end the Society's financial position was satisfactory with net assets sufficient to meet the Society's obligations.

INFLUENCING POLICY

The Society influences policy in a variety of ways, through conferences, issuing statements, lectures and responding to consultations. It has continued to make its views known to the public through press releases, media interviews, its website and by making much greater use of email.

Woodlands
The Society has called for a strategic look at Exmoor's woodlands in order to understand their full potential and the need for a new initiative that concentrates on woodland as a land use in its own right and integrated with the farmed landscape. It has taken the lead in partnership with the ENPA, the Forestry Commission, Natural England, the Woodland Trust and the Crown Estate to commission an independent report by September. Its recommendations, after consultation, will lead to an action plan.

ENPA Appraisal
The Society congratulated the ENPA on the successful outcome of a review into its performance and particularly the acknowledgement of the high quality of the work of the conservation section. The Society was concerned that the ENPA was overstretching itself especially with reduced staffing and government grant. It also raised issues about consultation, public relations and partnership working.

Exhibit at the Hope Bourne Exhibition, Dulverton Heritage Centre.

Hill Farming

The Society continues to be involved in campaigning for hill farming in two areas. First in helping to recognise the importance of the ecosystem services approach. These services are widely defined and include food and cultural services such as landscape quality, recreation and well-being as well as water quantity and quality, carbon sequestration and mitigation of climate change. Many of the services are provided by traditional livestock farming and the Society supports the drive for finding alternative sources for funding some of them. Payment for Ecosystem Services (PES) is being trialled on Exmoor through the Mires project. With funds from South West Water (SWW), drainage ditches are being blocked in order to rewet the peat, and the hydrological impact and other research work into archaeology and biodiversity are being monitored. So far SWW has not come up with a financial model of what it will pay farmers for storing the water even though rewetting peat has caused considerable costs to the farming business. The second area is the involvement of the Society in the debate on moorland management.

Exmoor Review

The Society's journal, of which we are now preparing the 55th volume, is an important source of information and influence on how people protect and enjoy Exmoor. Its editors have attracted high quality contributions covering aspects of Exmoor life from a variety of sources: some academic, some with great local knowledge, some with stories and memories.

The Local Plan

The Society is fully aware that the ENPA is in the process of producing its new local plan, which will determine planning policies for the next 10 to 20 years. So far the Society has been involved in the first round of consultations and will play a major part during the formal plan approval process.

PARTNERSHIPS

The Society recognises the value of partnerships and works with a wide range of public and voluntary bodies. It is represented on a wide variety of projects including the following:

- Moorland Board where the big issue has been swaling and where the Society has called for increased size of burns and more regular occurrence in order to catch up with the backlog of gorse, brambles and bracken. There are also concerns over stocking rates.
- Moorland Heritage Partnership (the Heart of Exmoor, which the Society chairs) where the Society has contributed to several projects including the moorland classroom, reaching out to the public and reconditioning the moorland and has supported a two-year extension bid to the HLF.
- Mires from the Moor Project, where the Society has supported the archaeological report and continues to press that payments are made to farmers for the services of

water quality, water retention and locking up carbon. So far SWW has not come up with a financial model of how it will support farmers.

- ENPA Consultative Forum, where a wide range of issues has been discussed.
- ENP Partnership (Management Plan) overview groups, where the Society is represented on the Landscape, Heritage, and Information and Education Groups.

PLANNING

The Society has continued to monitor all planning applications coming to the ENPA. Unlike previous years, there have been no applications for wind turbines. This may reflect the Government's decision to reduce the "feed in tariff" and if this is the case we might expect new applications now that the tariff has been increased.

The Society comments only on applications that could have a significant impact on the landscape character of the National Park. This year there have been four such occasions. After much deliberation and several site visits including one with members of the Authority the Society supported an application permitting a major redevelopment for Shearwell Data's site, near Wheddon Cross. Our only concerns were over a large Agricultural Building to be located at the end of the enlarged car park. It was our view that this building was too large and would have an adverse impact on the landscape. Although permission was granted for the development a revised application has subsequently removed this element.

We also found ourselves able to support an application for a new Doctors' Surgery in the corner of the playing field at Dunster. Here we took the view that, although it was within the Conservation Area its exact location and careful design ensured that it would not have a detrimental impact on the setting of the Castle Mound.

During the year there have been a number of applications for large and isolated agricultural buildings. Whilst the Society recognises the need for such buildings to house the livestock during the winter months, their siting needs to be chosen with extreme care and sensitivity. Such large buildings, particularly where they are on high ground, near roads and public rights-of-way, are likely to have a significant detrimental impact on landscape character. They are potentially less damaging when located close to existing buildings associated with the farmstead.

Sir Antony Acland, Society President, with the Lucy Perry Poetry Competition Award winners Emily Coles of Kingsmead School, Wiveliscombe (centre) and Ruby Winzer of Dulverton Middle School (right).

Because of our concerns the Society found it necessary to support recommendations for refusal by Officers for agricultural buildings near Lynton and Wheddon Cross. On both occasions the Officers' recommendations were supported by the Planning Committee and permission was refused.

EDUCATION, OUTREACH & AWARDS

The Society has continued to support the Exmoor Curriculum and at the same time has added several new approaches during the year:

Rachel Thomas with a visitor at the Hope Bourne Exhibition.

- The Pinnacle Award for business enterprise was presented to Alan and Oliver Hill in order to help their contracting business.
- The Lucy Perry Children's Poetry Award senior category winner was presented to Emily Coles and junior category winner Ruby Winzer.
- The Samuel Foss Conservation Award – two awards were presented: to Mr & Mrs Brian Coulson for their work on the Common Dormouse, and to Mike Jones for his work in documenting the industrial heritage of the Brendon Hills including the West Somerset Mineral Line.
- The Founder's Award was presented to Ruth Chambers in recognition of the work in helping the Society in policy and other matters as former Deputy Chief Executive & Head of Policy of the Campaign for National Parks.
- The Hope Bourne Adult Poetry Award was presented to Robert Miles.
- The Chris Binnie Water Award for Sustainable Water Management was presented to Guy Thomas-Everard for his hydro-scheme at Miltons, Dulverton.

EVENTS

The opening of the Hope Bourne Exhibition on 22 March at the Dulverton Guildhall Heritage and Arts Centre was an important event with a large turnout and much interest in the items displayed, the DVD, photographs and pictures reflecting Hope's love of Exmoor. Over the subsequent three months, visitor numbers to the Heritage Centre increased, and sales of the DVD, postcards and notelets have gone well.

The Society Conference, in partnership with the ENPA, attracted a full audience in Dulverton Town Hall. There was much interest in the subject of 'Exmoor's Rivers', and the speakers from the Environment agency, ENPA and West Country Rivers Trust answered lively questions from the floor. Charles Cowap as keynote speaker explained his work in developing payments for ecosystem services. The Chairman of the Society emphasised the importance of rivers for public enjoyment while recognising that there could be conflict between different users and the need to manage this.

There was much variety in the 2012-2013 Events Programme with over fifty walks, talks and other events, which included the annual Hazel Eardley-Wilmot celebration day. Noticeable was the interest about the Lorna Doone walk with the walk leader appearing in 'Countryfile' in January. Walks organised by Society Groups have added to a full programme of events including talks given by specialists, as well as the increasing number given by the Society. The Groups this year have grown in membership and attendance at their events, and continue to recruit new members for the Society.

Quotes from members as a result of the subscription increases:
"I am glad to be supporting the Exmoor Society and your good work in preserving this wonderful area."
"Still cheap at the price. Good Value."
"Good luck to the Society. It does a splendid job."

Hope Bourne Exhibition:
"An exhibition celebrating the work of an extraordinary woman."
"A rich legacy of drawings and paintings by the reclusive Exmoor character, Hope Bourne."

First Society walk of the 2013 season – walkers at the "lost" village of Clicket.